Caught Up into Heaven

Caught Up into Heaven

Marietta Davis

W Whitaker House

Publisher's note: This edition from Whitaker House has been updated for the modern reader. Words, expressions, and sentence structure have been revised for clarity and readability. Although the more modern Bible translation quoted in this edition was not available to the author, the Bible versions used was carefully and prayerfully selected in order to make the language of the entire text readily understandable while maintaining the author's original premises and message. The views stated by Marietta Davis are not necessarily those of the publisher.

Unless otherwise indicated, all Scripture quotations are taken from the *New King James Version*, © 1979, 1980, 1982, 1984 by Thomas Nelson, Inc. Used by permission. All rights reserved. Scripture quotations marked (KJV) are taken from the King James Version of the Holy Bible.

CAUGHT UP INTO HEAVEN

ISBN-13: 978-0-88368-575-4
ISBN-10: 0-88368-575-2
Printed in the United States of America
© 1999 by Whitaker House

Whitaker House
1030 Hunt Valley Circle
New Kensington, PA 15068
www.whitakerhouse.com

Library of Congress Cataloging-in-Publication Data

Davis, Marietta, 1823–1848.
Caught up into heaven / by Marietta Davis.
p. cm.
ISBN 0-88368-575-2 (trade paper)
1. Future life—Christianity. 2. Private revelations. 3. Davis,
Marietta, 1823–1848. I. Title.
BT833.D38 1999
248.2'9—dc21   99-28209

5 6 7 8 9 10 11 12 13 14 **WH** 15 14 13 12 11 10 09 08

Contents

Preface

❦

In the summer of 1848, a twenty-five-year-old woman named Marietta Davis fell into a deep sleep or trance for nine days. All endeavors on the part of her friends and physicians failed to arouse her from this unnatural state. When at last she awoke to a consciousness of external things, she was in full possession of all her natural faculties, with an almost supernatural acuteness of perception added beyond that.

Before she fell into the trance, she had been considerably troubled in regard to her future eternal state and was greatly disturbed by some lingering doubts. Her mother and sisters were exemplary members of a Baptist church in Berlin, New York, where they all resided, but Marietta's doubt seemed to have kept her from the enjoyment of the hope in which her family so confidently rested. But when she came out of the trance, it was with joy and rejoicing over the unspeakable things that she had seen and heard. Her mouth was filled with praises to God, and her heart swelled with gratitude to Him for His loving-kindness.

Marietta declared that while her body lay as if it were in death, her spirit had visited the eternal world. She informed her friends that she would not remain long with them but would soon return to that place to enjoy a mansion prepared for her in her heavenly Father's kingdom. After this she lived seven months, dying at the time she had predicted. So perfectly did she know the hour of her departure that, when it arrived, she selected a hymn and began to sing it with the family. While they sang, her spirit took its flight so gently that she did not attract their attention. Thus the hymn began with her friends on earth and was undoubtedly concluded with the angels in heaven.

As with any spiritual vision, experience, or prophecy, the narrative of Marietta Davis' experiences in the spiritual realm should be read thoughtfully and prayerfully, testing its words according to the whole of Scripture. (See, for example, 1 John 4:1; 1 Corinthians 2:15; 1 Thessalonians 5:21.) The tone of the narrative is reverent and gives glory to Jesus the Redeemer; therefore, it has had a spiritually uplifting effect on many of its hearers and readers. If read in the spirit in which it was given, it cannot fail to gladden and encourage the Christian and to lead one from thoughts of man's material existence to the world beyond. As you follow Marietta in her wide range of spiritual thoughts and visions, forgetting the outer world, you will find that the heavens are opened to your view, revealing their glory and magnificence.

chapter 1

Entering the
Heavenly Realm

❧

There are no means that can properly convey
to man, through his external senses, the
scenes I witnessed while my body lay in un-
conscious slumber. No medium of communication is
sufficiently clear to give the perfect outline of what
is invisible and incomprehensible to mortals. Words
are too cumbersome and meaningless, and human
utterance mars the beauty and perfection of heavenly speech and corrupts the purity of thoughts thus
conveyed. I am so aware of my utter inability to relate the facts of my experience that I am pained even
by the thoughts of attempting such a feat. However,
for the benefit of my fellowman, I do attempt it.

I had long before discovered the vanity of
earthly things, the imperfections of human associations, the unreliability of vast portions of religious
faiths and impressions, and the lack of permanent
peace in the disquieted soul of man. I earnestly desired to know more about the state we call immortality, for I knew that the outer world would perish.
As I meditated from day to day, and as I tried to determine the nature of the human soul, I became less
conscious of external things. My inner mind grew
stronger and more active, until the dim shadows of
the objects and interests of this busy life of mortals

ceased from my view, and my vision closed to the outer world.

Then objects new and strange appeared. I did not know that I was retiring from the world of sorrow and of human strife; nor did I understand that my spiritual vision was opening and that what I saw dimly moving before me was a reality, the dawning of an immortal life. I seemed to be departing from some former condition and launching out into a boundless sea. I seemed to be traversing unexplored regions, veiled in uncertain vision, and floating in midair over an immeasurable abyss below. Alone and unguided, my timid and uncertain spirit gladly would have returned to the land of shadows from which it had come.

A Heavenly Guide

Half-conscious of my condition, with dreamy thoughts, I seemed to ask, "Is there no one familiar with the journey I pursue to guide me in my movements through this trackless space?" All of a sudden, in the distance and above me, I saw a light descending, having the appearance of a brilliant star. All my perceptive powers were then concentrated until nothing was visible but the approaching light. As it advanced, its foreshadowing halo illuminated the expanse around me, and my exhausted being received new life from the invigorating glory that beamed upon it.

Gently I began to move. As I ascended, I drew nearer to the source of the light that gladdened and quickened my spirit. As I approached it, I began to discover the outline of what at first appeared to be a glorified human being. The figure gradually became more distinct until hovering in the atmosphere before and above me was an angel, whose excellence far exceeded the fairest image of my human thought. That form, more lovely than language has power to portray, moved silently as it drew near me.

She wore a crown made of clustered jewels. Her whole being reflected the light of celestial love. In her left hand was a cross, an emblem of meekness, innocence, and redeeming grace. In her right hand was a wand of pure intellectual light. With this she touched my lips, and like a flame of holy love, it quickened an immortal principle that diffused its enlivening spirit throughout my being.

A new kind of sensation awoke within me and, moving harmoniously, prompted a desire for companionship with the angelic being from whose hand came forth the stream of quickening light. I looked upon her, wishing to learn her name, when she spoke. The harmony of her utterance filled me with unknown delight. She said, "Marietta, you desire to know me. In my errand to you, I am called the Angel of Peace. I come to guide you to where those who are from earth exist. If you wish to profit from the lesson, follow me. But first behold your form in the world from which you have come."

There, far below me and through a dark and misty way, I beheld a sickly mortal body. Around it were gathered my anxious friends, employing every means to awaken it, but all in vain.

"Behold," said my glorious guide, "a picture of human life. There, tortured with sympathetic love, family members struggle to hold the crumbling vase and keep the flickering light from expiring. There, from youth to old age, rolls the tide of human woe. Death takes the tender and lovely human form and hides it from mortal sight. The flower that has gladdened everyone around it folds its leaves and withers at the touch of death. Earth, with her swarming millions, presents a mingled scene of rising hopes, ambition, strife, and death. Her inhabitants are dismayed by the approach and fear of Death, the cruel destroyer. Time quickly measures the fleeting moments of human existence, and generations follow generations in quick succession."

To this address I replied, "These thoughts are the burden of my young and inexperienced mind. This picture of human life that you have shown me has been in my thoughts night and day. This is the cause of my sorrow. Can you tell me in what portion of the universe human beings find a resting place when their spirits depart? Can you remove the veil that conceals them from mortal vision? Can you guide me to where they are? Oh, tell me, do they have a home, and may I go to where my loved ones have been carried?"

Man at the Point of Death

The Angel of Peace then said to me, "Do you desire to know the condition of the departed members of your race, and to be made familiar with the effects of the habits and associations of perverted man? In time you will know, but keep in mind that their conditions are varied." Then bidding me to look upward she said, "What do you behold?" Obedient, I looked above me and with wonder beheld an orb far brighter than the sun of earth in its noonday glory.

Pure light, beaming along the celestial skies, radiated from it.

"There," said my guide, "are many you would like to see who, clothed in raiment soft and white, move in harmony. There, night never arrives, and death and gloom have no place. Those who enjoy that blessed abode do not suffer; no sin or pain disturbs their calm repose. But you will learn more of this later on. Other scenes less joyous must first be given you. Marietta, you know well that men have varied characters. When their spirits depart from the unsettled and shattered habitation of earth below, no change occurs to their natures."

Then touching my forehead, again she said, "What do you see?" My vision was opened to a new scene, and I beheld before me forms without number, struggling in the agonies of death. Some were in kingly palaces on deathbeds richly hung with drapery of costly price. Some were in humble cottages; others were in gloomy prisons, in places of vice and iniquity, in lone forests, in barren deserts, and in deep and wild waters.

Some lay beneath the scorching sun; some were perishing upon bleak and snowy mountains; some were surrounded by weeping and attentive friends; others were dying alone and forgotten. Some were perishing for their religion; others were tortured by a cruel savage. Some were aged, despised, helpless, and forsaken; others were orphans, cast out and destitute. Some were dying from wounds inflicted by an assassin; others were crushed beneath the heavy tread of the warhorse in the battlefield.

Thus the place where time and eternity meet was revealed as a scene of indescribable misery.

"This," said my guide "is only a faint view of the effects of violated law."

Touched again by the light beaming from her right hand, I beheld the immortality of those who were leaving their houses of clay, entering into the regions of eternity, and commencing new and untried realities. Around each new spirit of the dead, other spirits of various appearances and movements were assembled.

I saw new spirits of the dead congregated over battlefields in an intermediate region or passageway to the spirit world. The arrival of these new spirits into the heavenly realm was eagerly anticipated by attending spirits who had the same moral nature as those who had just died. This is the case with all classes and conditions of men. All classes, as they emerge from the physical form, are attracted to and mingle with beings of similar character. Those of discordant and ungodly natures are attracted by like elements and enter into regions overhung with clouds of night; those who love what is good and who desire pure associations are conducted by heavenly messengers to the orb of glories appearing above the intermediate scene.

The strange sensations of human spirits as they mingled with the multitudes of other disembodied spirits, beholding what was transpiring around them, excited my wonder. While I was watching their movements, I began to ask myself if what I saw was a reality or a mere illusion resulting from a dreamy state. Upon discovering my thoughts, my guide took me by the hand and said, "These beings moving about you, once the inhabitants of earth, having left their mortal dwellings, are beginning a new state of existence. Their surprise is the effect of their sudden change from external objects to spiritual ones, and their more immediate knowledge of cause and effect. But when you are more able to understand, you will be shown more of this state and their condition. We will leave these scenes and ascend to the bright orb that you see in the distance." Having said this, my guide led me toward the cloud of light.

Outer Expanse of Paradise

While we were passing the intermediate scene, she touched me again, and I became conscious of additional and expanded vision. "Behold," said she, "the countless planetary hosts. Notice the rolling orbs, suns, and systems of suns, all moving in silence and harmony. The vast expanse is occupied and filled with universes, constructed in infinite wisdom. These are inhabited by holy beings, happy and immortal, though varied in degree of development and refined spirituality."

Again, my organs of perception were touched. Above and around me, and far in the distance, spirits of pure light were passing here and there as fast as a thought could cross one's mind.

"These," said my guide, "are ministering angels. Their supreme delight is to go upon errands of mercy. Their home is with the ever blessed. They are employed as guardian protectors and messengers of holy thought to those in conditions below them."

While I was beholding them ascend and descend, one drew near me. In his arms was an infant spirit. The angel passed, and I saw that the baby rested in

calm security, apparently conscious of its safety in
the hands of its protector. "From where did this
child come?" I inquired. The angel answered, "I received it from a heartbroken mother at the gateway
of death, as the child's spark of life expired in the
external world, and I am conveying it to the sphere
of infancy in the paradise of peace."

As the infant's guardian spirit proceeded, we
moved silently in the same direction, until the
scenes below vanished from my vision. My being was
absorbed in the bright light descending from the orb
that we were approaching. Soon we entered a plain
on which there were visible trees, each bearing fruit.
Their interwoven branches formed an arched canopy
of evergreen above us. Passing through these shad-
owy groves, I was delighted with the melody of the
birds, whose warbling notes arose in sweetest song.
There we paused. Supposing that I was on some terrestrial planet, I inquired its name.

My guide answered, "These trees, these flowers,
these birds occupy the outer expanse of the spiritual
paradise. So pure are they, and so refined, that mortals with beclouded vision may not behold them. And
so soft are their notes that they are not made audible to the dull hearing of men. Beings who inhabit
more earthly forms cannot imagine that such refined
natures exist. Absent from your body, you can comprehend through spiritual senses the existence and
reality of spiritual places, but what you now behold
is simply the outline and mere exterior of the home
of spiritual beings. These floral plains and warbling
melodies are only the lower order of the external
habitation of the sanctified.

"Do these groves appear as if they are moved with adoration? Do you see that these melodies that charm and invigorate you with new life are notes offered to higher degrees of love?

"When the redeemed leave the valley and shadow of death, they are first conducted here by their guardian protectors. Here they are taught the rudiments of immortal life and receive instructive lessons relating to their heavenly abode. Here they learn the nature of pure love, unmarred by sin. Here the instruments of ceaseless praise are first tuned, as they learn to utter immortal accents to the Lord, their Redeemer. Here they receive new thoughts that bring to them an increasing sense of the reality of their change.

"Here in these groves, friends who have advanced in spiritual attainments return from higher employment to welcome the spirit as it enters the spirit world. Here relatives are permitted to meet and converse, and it is in these immortal groves where spirits first attempt in unity the song of redeeming grace. Here, reposing in soft and heavenly sweetness, they first breathe the pure air of paradise."

While listening to this strange, though welcome, address, my spirit yearned to meet the friends long lost to me on earth. The angel said, "Your present mission is to learn the condition of the departed children of God; therefore, we must not delay. When your course on earth has ended and you are in the infancy of your immortal state, you will here mingle with your kindred and receive lessons that will prepare you for more exalted mansions and the more glorified home of the blessed."

Then she reached out her hand and plucked a rose that hung over us. Bidding me to smell its fragrance, she touched my lips with it. Again, a more interior sight was given. Around me and moving in every direction, and through the varied floral scenes, I beheld innumerable happy beings. Desiring to mingle with them, I sought permission, but my guide moved on and upward through the forests that became purer and fairer as we ascended.

chapter 2

The City of Peace

❧

A t a distance, on a higher plain, I saw a dome of light. "That," said my guide, "is the gateway leading to the City of Peace. There your Redeemer is made visible. Saints and angels abide there. On harps of gold and stringed instruments, with immortal lyres, they chant in alleluias the song of redemption, the song of peace, the song of undying love."

"May I enter there?" I inquired.

Again she touched my lips, and they moved, uttering praise in unaccustomed accents that melted into the harmony of celestial love.

As we drew near, a group of attendants even more glorious gathered around the gateway. The foremost one addressed my guide in language I could not understand. Music, the music of love, was in their conversation, and joy encompassed them like a halo as they welcomed us at the entrance of the Holy Sanctuary.

A gate of jasper, set with diamonds, opened, and two angelic beings approached. Taking me by each hand, they led my tremulous spirit toward an inner gate, a more immediate entrance to the pavilion of light.

Then I remembered my discordant state. Thoughts of my former sins, my doubts, and my

19

rebellious nature rushed upon my mind. Feeling entirely unprepared to endure the glory of those who now assembled, my spirit failed me.

Face to Face with the Savior

The angelic attendants then bore me in their arms along the portal to the feet of a Being most glorious. Upon His head was a crown of pure light, and over His shoulders hung golden locks. His loveliness can never be expressed.

"This, Marietta," said an attending angel, "is your Redeemer. For you, He *'suffered outside the gate'* (Heb. 13:12) in incarnation. For you, having *'trodden the winepress alone'* (Isa. 63:3), He died." Awed by His goodness, tenderness, and love, I bowed, feeling that I would worship Him if I were worthy to do so.

Reaching forth His hand, He raised me up. In a voice that filled my soul with inexpressible delight, He said, "Welcome, My child. Daughter, spirit of a race forlorn, enter for a season the portals of the redeemed." Then addressing the surrounding beings, He continued, "Receive this your companion spirit." Just then the worshipping congregation arose as upon the breath of holy love and meekly welcomed me as an heir of grace. With tuned instruments, the immortal choir began a welcoming chant:

> Worthy is the Lamb who has redeemed us! Exalt His name, all you who are sanctified. Adore Him, you cherubim who worship in the celestial heavens. Adore Him, for He has

exalted us. We will praise His name, the name of our God Most High.

We will bow down and worship at His feet. We will sing of His loving-kindness. Oh, you breezes of immortal love, carry His name throughout the universe of worshipping beings! For our sister is exalted from the depths of iniquity, and we receive her from the hands of our Prince and Savior. Utter alleluias to Him forever, all you adoring hosts. Utter His praise forever.

The music of this soft and melodious utterance moved like the voice of many waters (see Revelation 14:2), filling the entire dome. As the anthem closed, the echo departed into the distance, as though carried from wave to wave along the holy atmosphere.

The spirit of praise so inspired each chorister with the fullness of divine melody that, moved by it, they softly touched the silver chords of their golden harps. Each note reverberated as if gliding along the sensitive nerves of spirit hearts, components of one immortal lyre. Each measure of music, like noiseless waves, swelled over that sea of angelic beings. I seemed to be moving with their gentle undulations, when a spirit from the innumerable company approached me and, addressing me in a familiar manner, called me by name.

A Visit with Departed Loved Ones

The spell of music being broken, I was surprised to find myself in the embrace of one whom, on earth,

I had loved with the affection of an infant soul. I willingly sank into her arms, and with a sister's tenderness she pressed me to her immortal form, saying, "Sister spirit, welcome, for a season, to our home of peace."

"Thrice welcome!" uttered the music of a thousand voices. With them were gathered those I loved, many old and familiar friends, all eager to greet me and receive me to their kind embrace. In the spacious room around us were seats in the form of an amphitheater, glorious beyond description. We sat here.

Although I knew these friends well on earth, their appearance had changed. Each was now an embodiment of intellect unassociated with the physical form in which I had known them before. Not having the means to convey their nature exactly, I can only say that they appeared to be all mind, all light, all glory, all adoration, all love supremely pure, all peace and calm serenity, all united in sublime employment, all expressions of heavenly, unfolding joy.

They conversed freely, but they did not use the language of human beings. When they spoke, no audible sound followed, yet thought moved with thought, and spirit was familiar with spirit. Ideas associated with their heavenly lives flowed from being to being, and soon I learned that in heaven there is no concealment; nothing is hidden. Harmony of soul, harmony of desire, harmony of speech, harmony in the swelling notes of adoring anthems, harmony in instructive movement, harmony in increasing thought—such harmony was their life, their love, their manifestation, and their supreme delight.

Again with harps tuned in unison of praise, and in an ascending octave, they chanted a hymn to their Maker's name. My guide urged me to unite in the animating song of redemption. I could not join them, being absorbed in the contemplation and glory of this long-sought home of rest. When they closed that sacred hymn, my guide, touching my lips again with the wand of light, invited me to mingle, as a companion, among the members of this divine abode.

Being after being pressed immortal lips to mine and seemed anxious to fold me in their arms. As though I were a newborn soul, they caressed me, after looking up in thankfulness to their Redeemer and their Lord.

"Is this heaven?" my spirit said. "Are these happy souls those who once struggled in forms of clay? Are these immortal faces, radiant with the glory of this resplendent mansion, the spiritual faces of those I once saw in careworn life? Where has their age and decrepitude gone?"

I have often listened to earthly teachers who labored to convey some faint idea of immortal life. I have seen them obviously grieving when they realized that their efforts were ineffective on most minds. I have asked, Can heaven be so glorious? Have you not painted an exaggerated picture of it? Can man, if he attains that blessed abode, bask in the sunbeams of such supreme delight? Surely, the highest thoughts of man fail to approach the reality and the delights of that heavenly scene!

Caught Up into Heaven

The Pilgrim's Address

Then approached one whom on earth I had seen bending tremulously over a pilgrim's staff. I knew it was someone familiar, someone old and wasted away, whose gray-haired head once told the story of a life of woe. Now full of immortal youth, the spirit of this person stood before me. No staff was there, no trembling frame, no grief-worn cheek, no hollow eye, no sickly form; but light, health, and vigor were manifest.

This pilgrim spirit said to me, "Behold in me the effectiveness of redeeming grace. This heart was once the cage of unholy thoughts. These hands were employed in sin. These feet moved swiftly along the downward road that led to sorrow and death. The body in which I used to live was corrupt, worn with grief, and dying of disease. But now, all hail that name Immanuel! Through Him, I am redeemed; through Him I wear garments of light and exist in immortal youth. I now sing, 'O death, where is thy sting? O grave, where is thy victory?' (1 Cor. 15:55 KJV). Worthy is the Lamb who offered Himself to redeem! Worthy—oh, give Him adoration, you countless hosts, you innumerable throng! Worship and adore Him, all you angels! Indeed, let universes adore! Adore Him, for He is worthy to receive anthems of universal praise!"

While he was uttering this psalm, the people in the great expanse united, lifting on high an immeasurable volume of divine notes. Then appeared a company of children who, hand in tiny hand, moved around and chanted with their infant voices, "Praise Him, for while He was on earth He said,

'Let the little children come to Me, and do not forbid them' (Matt. 19:14)."

The Glory of the Cross

When this new song had ended, there descended a light surpassing any that had been witnessed before. As I looked on, the dome above me parted, and beings far more glorious approached. Awed by the presence of the light, and desiring to flee before it, I approached my guide.

Before I could speak, she said to me, "What you have seen, Marietta, is only the promise of joys to come. Here you have been welcomed, and here you have witnessed this particular manifestation of your Redeemer and the harmony of this entrance to the divine abode. But behold! Above you the descending glory of the cross appears. Redeemed spirits, members of your race who have advanced to higher life, are watching. Witness the foreshadowing of the glory of the Seventh Sphere. These angels wait on you."

Then, above me, a cross appeared in the midst of twelve others. On it were the words *Patriarchs, Prophets, and Apostles.* Above it was written, "Jesus of Nazareth, King of the Jews."

Bowing at the feet of the cross was a spirit whose garments were white and whose expression was one of holy adoration. She kissed the cross, and then descended, approaching me. In musical speech superior to all the anthems to which I had listened with wonder and delight, she said, "Welcome, spirit from the world of woe. By the will of Jesus, even Jesus who was crucified, my Lord and Redeemer, I come to commune with you. 'Tis only by His permission that you are admitted here. Though you will be required to return to your friends on earth, do not be sad."

The thought of being again subjected to the sins and misfortunes of my former life so affected me that it seemed as if I were leaving the divine abode and rapidly descending to earth. But just then I was embraced by my guide, who said, "When you return, you will go to bear a message of holy love to the earth. After that, at an appointed time, free from the power of mortal attachments, you will enter here as a member of the holy assembly."

The spirit who descended from the cross then said, "What you see, and the message I give you, you will unfold to my mortal son, who is yet struggling in the valley of night. In dove-like form, bear from eternity the olive branch of truth. Press it to his heart, and it will bud and blossom and, after much conflict, bear the ripened fruit.

"Marietta, you have been conducted here for a wise purpose. For this reason, I am permitted to instruct you in many things pertaining to earth and heaven. The thought of returning to earth makes you sad, yet you will go back laden with riches—the riches of instructive truth, the seeds of which will prepare the way for greater light.

"First learn that all heaven reveres the cross. Earth's religions are but dreamy scenes compared to these heavenly scenes. The highest thoughts of the human mind are vague and imperfect in comparison with our condition here. The spiritual heaven begins in perfect order just above the plains of earth. Around it move the guardian spirits. Countless guardian angels are mingling, as permitted, with the inhabitants of earth. No day, hour, or moment passes when each mortal is not watched by the spirit appointed to his charge.

"Man does not know the nature of sin or the fullness of grace in his redemption. He will not believe, even though angels have gathered around him to tell the story of immortality. Innumerable causes prevent the light of heaven from reaching and controlling the race of man, which is moving toward wretchedness and death. But the time draws near when man will become more conscious of the reality of this heavenly abode; his attention will be turned more fully to the truth of the inner life. Man's redemption draws near. Let angels amplify their hymns, for soon the Savior descends with holy, attending angels."

This spirit then led the heavenly sounds of an immortal hymn too full and too harmonious in movement to be transmitted by human language. At its close she said, "Sister spirit, rest in the embrace of holy affection. Observe what passes around you, for upon your mind will be mirrored a faint and remote expression of the joy that fills this land of peace. When I descended, you will remember, I kissed the cross. All saints delight themselves in thus expressing their remembrance and regard for their Redeemer who offered Himself as a sacrifice."

During the pause that then ensued in her address, voices arose, apparently in the distance, in soft and melodious alleluias. The accents moved like living beings, seeking to wake the song of redemption in every spirit throughout the vast gathering.

"Who are these?" I inquired.

"These are the ones who," she said, "having come out of great tribulation (see Revelation 7:13–15), cease not day or night to raise their anthems high in exaltation of their Savior's name. The heaven of heavens is animated with this celestial love. From earthly saints, who through pathways of ascending life humbly adore and sing of redeeming grace, the soul-inspiring melody of heavenly adoration is borne on high. Above you, you will discover beings of higher attainment moving in eternal light.

"Do you wish to dwell forever in this world of peace, joy, and divine love? Will you bear some humble part with the psalms of these immortal choristers? Remember your former doubts, your lack of faith and consecration, for only in Christ the Redeemer can you attain an inheritance in this blessed abode."

This last address revived within me remembrance of my former doubts, my lack of confidence in the Savior, and my lack of consecration to His cause. My spirit drooped. I saw the justice of the mild reproof and inquired, "May I yet hope? Or is the opportunity to secure this heaven of life forever gone? I would gladly give myself, my all. I would gladly return no more to earth. Oh, that I could forever dwell where peace flows gently like a river and where love moves unpolluted from heart to heart!"

"Be faithful then," said the spirit, "to the light that has been given to you, and at last you will enjoy the bliss of heaven. Marietta, the scene now passing before you is one laden with interest. In this assembly are the prophets and martyred saints. See, their garments are white—pure and transparent. Upon their hearts is the manifestation of the cross. In their left hands are golden censers, and in their right hands are small volumes."

The scene expanded, and I saw, arising from the center, a pyramid composed of pearls and precious stones. The multitudes were congregated around it. It was set with crosses of heavenly diamond, upon which were engraved the names of those who had suffered for their love of truth and who, not considering their lives dear, had endured persecution even unto death (Rev. 12:11). Upon the pyramid stood three spirits in the attitude of meekness and adoration. In their hands and above them, they held a cross, from which floated an ever unfurling banner.

"These," said my guide, "are the chosen: one patriarch, one prophet, and one apostle. They represent the triune circle of angels who will attend the reappearing of the Son of Man and will go forth in the day appointed, gathering together the elect from the uttermost parts of the earth to the uttermost part of heaven. (See Mark 13:26-27.) The volumes that the spirits hold in their hands unfold the order of creation, the redemption of man, and the principles that govern the obedient—world without end."

chapter 3

The Infant Paradise

As the former scene closed upon my view, the spirit who had kissed the cross raised her hand, radiant with the light of life, and two children drew near. As they approached, they bowed gracefully and, each placing a hand in hers, looked with meekness into her lovely face and smiled.

Addressing me, she said, "These children left the earthly form while in their infancy and, being innocent, were conducted to the paradise of innocence in the Seventh Sphere—a state of moral purity and intellectual harmony."

The eldest of the two children, thus introduced, said, "Marietta, I rejoice to commune with you, since you will return to those who loved us and who mourned our departure from the valley of death. When you are again conversing with mortals, say to those who now sit by your earthly body that we have learned that though parents may grieve for us, ours is a cup overflowing with gladness to the spirit made free.

"Marietta, this is the world we know. Here we first awoke to the reality of our existence. We sometimes visit earth, conducted by our guardian angels, but it is unlike heaven. There we witness sorrow, pain, and death; here, harmony, happiness, and life abide."

The child then looked down as if in deep meditation, and all was silent. I thought the subject that had engaged his mind had made him sad, but soon I saw that his attitude was brought about by the approach of an angel who had passed just above us. Oh, how my being was affected by the sight! Light surrounded this angel like a well-formed garment. Her very movement was the harmony of harmonies. I desired to follow and said to the spirit who had kissed the cross, "Tell me, who is this so glorious? I feel her sacred influence and ardently desire to enjoy the society and the abode of such beings."

"This," said the spirit, "is an angel who belongs to the infant paradise. Have you not read in the Gospel the blessed expression of the Redeemer, *'In heaven their angels always see the face of My Father who is in heaven'* (Matt. 18:10)? This angel is the guardian of infants and is commissioned to meet infant spirits as they leave the external world and enter into the spiritual. She pauses in her ascension for you. She holds out her arms, and what do you see, Marietta?"

"A small, dim light," I answered.

The angel then breathed upon this light, as if imparting life to it, and pressed it to her heart in fondness infinitely above that manifested by earthly mothers. I saw that the small light was an infant, whose little spirit was now at rest. Feeling the heaven that encompassed and pervaded the angel, again I wished to fly away and, with the infant, be forever blessed. But while I was struggling to ascend, the angel arose—one flash of light, and she disappeared.

Caught Up into Heaven

An Earthly Perspective

Then a far different scene was revealed to me. Below me, in a little room, I saw a female kneeling by the lifeless body of her departed child. She convulsed, and at times tears streamed from her eyes. Then her face became like marble, her eyes set and glassy, and her whole form quivered while she pressed kiss after kiss upon the cold cheek of her lost babe. At this juncture, a man dressed in black gravely entered. The group gave way, and he silently approached the weeping mother. Taking her by the hand, the man said, "Sister, arise. *'The LORD gave, and the LORD has taken away; blessed be the name of the LORD'* (Job 1:21). Jesus said, *'Let the little children come to Me, and do not forbid them; for of such is the kingdom of heaven'* (Matt. 19:14). *'For I say to you that in heaven their angels always see the face of My Father who is in heaven'* (Matt. 18:10)."

Next I saw the mother sitting beside a coffin in an earthly gathering. Her eyes were fixed on the ceiling. Her countenance wore an expression of despair. Before the coffin stood the man whom I had seen enter the room of death. He read a psalm, offered prayer for the afflicted, and then encouraged the mourners by endeavoring to prove from the sacred text that the babe, though dead, would live again, and that an angel had conveyed it to Abraham's bosom.

The assembly disappeared, and one of the two children standing before me began to speak. To me he said, "The lifeless form in the vision was the representation of my own body. The weeping mother was my own mother. The scene was what transpired when I left that body; the man was the minister of a congregation in the outer world. The angel who paused while passing us was the bright spirit who conveyed me far above the influence of evil to a place prepared for delicate infants, where appointed spirits are ever occupied in nourishing infant minds. Do you wish to visit that nursery?"

As I expressed my interest in visiting that place, he looked up to the spirit as if to ask permission to conduct me there.

Artistry and Order

In a moment we were ascending in the direction of the angel who had carried along the infant and who had disappeared in the light. Soon we drew near what at first had appeared to be a city built in the midst of a plain full of flowers. There appeared stately edifices and streets lined with trees whose foliage cast a lovely shade. On the branches of these trees, birds of all colors appeared, and although all were singing with different notes, they mingled in one full and perfect harmony. Many corresponded to those on earth and yet were as superior to them as paradise itself was superior to the mortal world.

As we advanced, the beauty and harmony increased, and new scenes appeared. The architecture of the edifices, the sculptures in the open air, the fountains that sparkled in the light, the trees that waved their extended branches, the flowers and flowering vines became more majestic, interwoven, and beautiful. Also many avenues, each of which slightly ascended, led to a common center toward which we went.

Before me stood a vast and complicated structure whose outer walls and towers appeared to be formed of marble that seemed to be as delicate as snow. This served as the foundation of a vast canopy, like a dome, though far too extended to be expressed by the earthly architectural meaning of the term. We drew near this building, and I perceived that the dome was suspended over the vast circular space. "This," said my guide, "is the place where all infants from your globe are gathered for the instruction and support of their infant natures. Recall that you saw buildings on either side as we moved along the avenues. Each of these corresponds to what mortals call a nursery for the young. Infants are first conducted there and are nourished beneath the smile of their guardian angels. Though somewhat varying, each building is a miniature version of this vast temple of instructive manifestation. Each is a home for the infant spirits who enter there, until they attain higher degrees and enter the paradise of more advanced youthful existence. Then they will receive instruction adapted to a more intellectual condition.

"You see, Marietta, that no two buildings are perfectly alike in interior beauty, external form, or decoration, but that all combine harmoniously. Also, you can see that each guardian angel is different in the radiative light and individuality of the face and form. This you are permitted to know.

"Whenever an infant dies on earth, the guardian angel who bears up the spirit to the Land of Peace perceives its mind and, accordingly, groups the infant with others of similar intelligence. Just as a skillful gardener on earth directs the growth of the various species of the lily in one part of his garden, and roses in another part, and in another the camellias or the honeysuckles, so does angelic wisdom here classify the infant spirits according to their artistic, scientific, and social tendencies. Then each infant is assigned a home best adapted to the unfolding of his or her intellectual, artistic, and vocational harmony.

"Over each building preside seven guardian angels, each of whom directs a subordinate group of more youthful spirits who perform duties assigned to them, according to their type of being. And each of these, in turn, presides over a separate class of infant beings. This is the harmonious system of heavenly instruction.

"These buildings are arranged in families of sevens. In this way, each separate palace of instruction, which is situated in its own separate gardens and enclosures, is one of seven of similar variety and of like degree. In turn, seven of these families of seven palaces form the subordinate divisions of a more complex and magnificent temple, whose center pavilion is adapted to instruction in more exalted degrees of paradisical truth.

"The center palace of each ward is thus a magnificent temple of instruction, encircled in artistic splendors and floral harmonies, corresponding to its degree. This is surrounded by seven lesser pavilions of architectural beauty, encircled by corresponding adornments adapted to their subordinate but exalted conditions. And each of these last is also the center of a lesser group of buildings, also adorned with stately forms of blooming and sculptured perfection. In these last buildings, the infants dwell and are led forth each day to the superior palaces and to the center pavilion for the education of their unfolding natures.

"As soon as these infants rise to a degree suitable for the general assembly in the great and center dome, or temple of instruction, they are led first from their homes to their separate center schools. Then all emerge from the different wards and move beneath a cloud of angel choristers, who chant loud alleluias to their Prince and Savior. With the harmony of these angels, the infants move toward the outer temple."

The Paradisical Nursery

As the spirit grew silent, I saw on our right a portion of one of the lesser temples move aside, as if an invisible hand were pulling back a suspended curtain. To my already astonished spirit, there suddenly appeared the interior of one of the nurseries, supremely lit with glory and adorned with artistic beauty that corresponded to the majestic appearance of the infant paradise. At first I was greatly abashed, feeling my own unfitness to behold any abode so pure, lovely, and majestic. "There," I unconsciously uttered, "is heaven." My reflections were perceived by my instructress, who said, "Marietta, behold the manifestation of infant life in paradise. Let us enter, and there you will learn the true condition of those who as babes leave the world of sorrow, and who are immediately conveyed to this place and are thereafter happy.

"Mortals know little of the blessedness attending their little ones who leave in the morning of their existence. Those who believe in Christ become reconciled to the loss, but this is mostly dependent on the law of submission established in the Christian's heart. I was once a mother in the world of sorrow and loss. There I learned to weep, and there I also learned the priceless value of faith in God's mercy through our Lord Jesus Christ. There, Marietta, did I bid good-bye to the infants who lived only to pain a mother's heart at their parting.

"Three times I pressed to my fond heart my beloved babes—flesh of my flesh, bone of my bones, and life of my life—and looking up to God, adored Him for the precious gifts. But scarcely had I done this before, like young and tender buds, they were nipped by the frost of death, and I was left wounded and forlorn. I hoped in Jesus and left my babes to His care, believing that they were well. But Marietta, had I only known, if only I could have seen what you now see, then my soul would have had greater rest by the knowledge added to my faith. For here in this paradise, the babe who has left his parents in woe awaits their arrival, and here the babe is safe from the contamination of the vices and sins of the fallen race. See, Marietta," she continued, "these seeds of immortality."

I looked, and the interior that was opened before me was that of a temple gloriously adorned. In circular tiers, one rising above another, were segments of circles, each worked in gold and overshadowed by a seraph. In each tier an infant spirit was at rest. Before each infant was a guardian angel, whose duty it was to equip the spirit for its eternal existence in holy usefulness. The angel breathed upon it, and every breath caused its capacity and life to expand. The breath was that of holy love and inspiration, for the life of each angel was in God, whose quickening Spirit pervades all angels in the heavens.

As we entered, I saw that those infants, as they awoke to still greater consciousness and as they beheld their angel bending over them, wore an expressive smile and were happy.

If I could portray to you this one nursery and so fix it in your mind that you could realize its glorious magnificence, then I would be more content; but I cannot. No means are given me; no mortal can know the full extent of this place. If you could enter there with me, you would behold in the center, held in an angel's hand, a cross of pure and heavenly gold. On either side of the space, you would see maternal spirits directing youthful maidens while employed with the newly arrived infant spirits committed to their charge.

From the silken, cradle-like resting places, which were adorned with blossoms of every hue and overshadowed by the seraphim, those who had been received from bereaved parents were constantly arising. As they arose, they floated as with wings of pure light amid the moving angels. From the angels who conducted them, they learned to move and to observe the nature and employment of the family of spirits who watched over them. Each angel also had many forms of external imagery by which to impress the first principles of truth upon the minds of these infants, in a way that matched their bodies and minds.

There were also angels appointed who touched, in softest notes, the varied instruments upon which music is made. This music is ever mingling with angelic voices of sweet and heavenly utterance. The dome of the infant paradise is so constructed as to echo, in gentle undulations, each strain that appears to move with the life of the place. So soft, sweet, and melodious was this music that it gave action and strength to the spirits of those who were resting beneath the smiles of their guardians.

"This," said the spirit who had conducted me there, "is only one of many of these great temples and corresponds to all others on this level of instruction. Oh, that earthly parents could realize that this is the birthplace of those who are taken from the outer form when understanding has not yet awakened within them! From this place they ascend to other places prepared for them. But, Marietta, you have not witnessed the most delightful of all the realities connected with this temple."

chapter 4

Infants Received by the Savior

❖

As my guide spoke, each of the guardian angels arose with the infant of her charge and hovered in the great space of the infant nursery. These joined with a galaxy of choirs around the angel who held the cross. Instantly, a light infinitely superior to that in the temple descended from above. I was awed by the dignified presence of a group of angels, in whose midst was the glorious Being who was my Redeemer.

As this group approached the center of the nursery, the manifestation of the cross disappeared before the greater light. The angels paused, and the Being whom they attended smilingly said, *"Let the little children come to Me, and do not forbid them"* (Matt. 19:14). The sweetness and gentleness of the expression, and the love that shone from His face as these words moved from His lips, overcame me, and I sank at the feet of my heavenly conductor, who raised me up and drew me to herself.

I wish that the world could see and hear what then occurred. As the Redeemer spoke, those guardian angels drew near and presented Him with their treasures. He moved His hand above them, and goodness, like dew drops, fell from His hand. The infants appeared to drink as from a fountain of living water. They were blessed. The emanation from that Being was the water of life. The temple seemed to become a new place.

As the scene was closing, the angels who attended my Redeemer played upon stringed instruments and sang of redemption. He moved His gracious hand as if in acceptance of what the guardian angels had done, and they all bowed and veiled their faces in the garment of glory that encompassed them.

Suddenly, music, like the voice of many waters, arose from every temple in that great city. As the utterance moved forth in one swelling wave of angelic song, that Being, with those who had accompanied Him, reascended, and the angels of this temple resumed their former movement.

"This," said my guide, "is only the simpler portion of the heavenly exercises connected with preparing infant spirits for their enlarged capacity and useful employment. This is only part of the pleasing occupation of those who are appointed to rear these infant souls.

"Marietta, if man had not departed from purity and harmony, and therefore from affinity and companionship with beings of an exalted nature, the earth would have been a proper nursery for newborn spirits. But sin has separated the condition of the sinner from that of angels, for by it his moral nature was changed. Angels are pure. No stain is found upon them; no evil desires ever awaken improper energies within them. From them emanates life in its pure element.

"But those who are at variance with God are severed from the affinity of more exalted natures.

41

They have lost the relationship that blends them with the harmonious laws and beings of celestial order. Men, while in the darkness of their sinful condition, do not know what they have lost in this, and therefore they do not properly realize the necessity and benefit of a Savior. Only the Redeemer can restore the lost affinity.

"Thus the great truth of redemption is manifested to the infant spirits. Those who are mature are enabled to understand the law of salvation, even life in Christ. By means of this knowledge, they are led to acceptable adoration of Him who is their Redeemer.

"You will recall that, as He who blessed these little ones ascended, all the nurseries of this great city chanted united praises to God and the Lamb. This adoration was spontaneous. Those who know the consequences of sin are well prepared to behold the infinite mercy and condescension of Jesus and to adore Him from their innermost beings. When He moves in their midst, they inwardly utter songs; and as He is withdrawing from them, these songs assume outward expression. Marietta, these happy beings could not refrain from such a full manifestation of joy and thanksgiving any more than life could cease to flow from Him who is the Author of life.

"It is the same throughout all of heaven. Do you not realize that each breath of those beings around you is but a separate volume of praise to God?

"If men in the body knew the goodness of God in redemption, they would cease from evil and learn righteousness and the ways of peace. Marietta, do you understand this?"

I felt the reproof, knowing my former disbelief in salvation through Jesus. I gladly would have hidden my spirit from the scrutiny of that spirit who thus addressed me. I knew I had doubted the immortality of the soul and man's restoration from evil through the Lord Jesus Christ. And now I beheld that He is *"all and in all"* (Col. 3:11), the Source of every pure and holy delight, and the theme of all I had been permitted to see in the world of spirits.

This is the lesson that all the redeemed in heaven study with supreme delight and that inspires them with love too great for expression. While I seek to describe it to you, I feel both my own inability to express the ecstatic fullness of that holy passion, and the weakness of human language to declare the sense of that love.

As soon as the angels had resumed their former positions, my guide informed me that those infant spirits who had just been blessed by the Redeemer had been given into the charge of other angels who would gently train their minds through means suitable to them.

New Arrivals

Now was approaching a scene in which I would witness the reception of infants just arriving from earth. Above and around me, I saw angels hovering in the serene atmosphere, awaiting with their treasures the moment when they could enter the temple. While the former angels had given up their charges and were preparing to receive another group of infants from the earth, this new group of angels entered and occupied the center around the cross.

At first their movement was irregular but not disordered. Then the softest and gentlest music began, as if harmony had awakened from a sacred stillness and moved in almost silent utterance, like a breath from the heart of gentleness and love. I was surprised at the quiet movement of this sweet music and felt an impatient desire for some angel to touch the swelling notes and open up the melody that appeared to be suppressed.

But my guide relieved me by directing my attention to a company of maternal spirits who were gathering around those angels who had just entered. These moved to the time and serenity of the music while engaging with each angel in nourishing the infants they held. The music and movement of these maternal spirits manifested great caution. Meanwhile, all others in the temple were motionless, as far as I could discern, except three spirits who appeared to hover above the center. From these three, a soft and pure light radiated.

My guide explained, "These angels, encompassed in greater light than that of the temple, are of a higher and more exalted nature. From them proceeds a halo of superior light. This light is the descending life of love. Do you see how it concentrates, forming a separate spiral-like embodiment, encompassing and overshadowing those germinal existences in the arms of the guardian angels? Each angel nourishes a spirit whose being is just beginning and who, by reason of nature's violated laws, has been separated prematurely from its infant form in the external world. This soft music thrills every fiber of the being.

"Meanwhile, the Supreme Spirit is reorganizing the being of the infant spirit and giving it enlarged capacity—fitting each organ to its fellow organ in the harmony of perfection. Thus, tone and proper energy are established in the infant's system. The descending life-light enters the senses of the infant and then breathes out as the breath of life and the soul of love. The quickening Spirit gives energy to the life principle that is unfolding, so that the intellect may perceive, the judgment operate, the understanding embrace realities, and the being enjoy the life thereof."

Infants Restored to Harmony

Again I was touched with a stream of light, by which I was enabled to see each infant as a complex and exceedingly delicate instrument. Each separate portion of the infant body had movement but not purpose; each appeared to lie in a sort of spasm-like action, as if prompted by an energy not innate but applied. The movement was indefinite but kept increasing in force, until each organ appeared as if it were a separate, living being composed of its own organs.

This wonder of wonders overwhelmed me. In my surprise, I impulsively inquired, "Is this a real being?" No answer being given, I continued to address my guide, saying, "At first I saw in the angel's arms the life-germ of an infant form. This germ was so delicate that I could not comprehend how its guardian spirit could save the flickering flame of its life.

Then I saw, descending from above, a light that encompassed and pervaded the infant spirit. The infant then moved as if receiving life and energy. I saw the distinct organs of that infant, and then they were severed. Now, kind angel, I behold each organ appears to be its own living being and a distinct embodiment. Tell me, how will these varied, complicated, and disconnected parts unite again in harmony? How will they proceed? How will they be able to perform their functions in the greater structure?"

Again light encompassed my spirit, and its brightness penetrated the secret chambers thereof. Exquisite perceptions were awakened in me, and a new being of my own appeared to arise and look out upon the scene. Here I saw that countless spirit-functions existed in paradise, each responding to the touch of some invisible power. Being prompted, these functions embraced each other like animate and intellectual beings. As if moved by understanding, they joined together in perfect adaptation and harmony. As they embraced, they coalesced and became one distinct being, full and perfect.

In a similar manner, each infant organ that had been encompassed within the light of the three angels above, arose and embraced and so coalesced that there was no longer any distinction among them. My soul uttered unconsciously, "Praise Him for His mighty works!" for my spirit looked upon an infant in all the perfection of heavenly life. Yes, it was now an infant restored. I had perceived it as a flickering candle, then as a complex instrument unstrung, and then encompassed and pervaded by the sphere of life from the angels above.

What had been in disarray and at variance was now a well-tuned instrument in the form of a heavenly spirit. As it looked up into the faces of the angels, it smiled. That smile spoke of both intelligence and harmony. Truly, I thought, here is the essence of the verse, *"Do not marvel that I said to you, 'You must be born again'"* (John 3:7). From what had passed before me, I felt the force of that beautiful expression of David when he said, *"I am fearfully and wonderfully made"* (Ps. 139:14).

Turning to my guide, I inquired, "Is this real? Is this a redeemed spirit? Is this process absolute in the restoration of a soul born of discordant elements?"

"Truly," said my guide, "what you have seen is real. The movement and power of grace upon these spirits, whose sin puts them at variance with God, are hereby unfolded to your understanding. Marietta, the light descending from angels could not restore, the music could not harmonize, the guardian angels could not supply what had been lost. Their duty was to support the external form while this dissevering process took place and while the components were restored and adapted for proper use by Him who is the Redeemer. He alone has the power to tune each fiber of the being, to purify, and to breathe the life of holiness into the soul, giving new life, energy, inclination, and love. Only He can bring about their reunion, resulting in perfect life in the infant form.

"You look upon a spirit at the end of its redemption. This spirit is now prepared to rest in the soft and balmy bed of repose from which you have seen others rise to higher life. Marietta, treasure this in your soul, but remember that it is only one nursery of infant life that you have seen. Each temple in the expanse has been equally occupied with infants."

As the scene changed, my guide continued: "Listen, Marietta. The melody of angels moves upon the holy atmosphere of the city. They chant praises to God and to the Lamb for the infants' redemption, for great is the number of these spirits restored to the harmony of perfect beings. For this reason, Marietta, thanksgivings are offered to our heavenly Parent at each closing scene. These thanksgivings bring the newborn spirit into the harmony and the possession of heaven."

Oh, how my spirit rose in ascending praise, adoration, and glory, inexpressible and divine! As the Revelator said, it was *"like the voice of many waters"* (Rev. 14:2).

The whole city seemed to resolve itself into the voice of praise. "Oh, is this heaven?" I asked. "How blessed it is to be considered worthy to enter the city of God! And this is only the infant paradise; this is only the song uttered by this group of infant spirits in view of their restoration to harmony and heaven. How vast and incomprehensible must be the expression of thanksgiving when redemption is complete, when the bride, the Lamb's wife, arises from the Marriage Supper in that Great Day when God will make up His jewels!" (See Malachi 3:17.)

The bliss was so entrancing that I felt like ascending with the divine praises. But reflections upon my unworthiness overcame me, and I fell into the holy arms of my guide.

chapter 5

Christic Suffering
on the Cross

❦

As I lay in the arms of my heavenly guide, I
looked into her face, which wore an expression of deep emotion. With earnestness her
eyes were fixed above, and her holy lips moved as if
in prayer. At first the expression of her features was
so sorrowful that I thought she would weep, but
tears would have been a feeble manifestation of the
feeling that I could plainly see continued to increase.
I said to myself, "Do angels grieve? Can sorrow enter
this Holy City?"

The music had ceased, but its echo reverberated
and moved in the distance. Silence reigned in the
vast expanse. I still leaned upon my blessed protector, anxiously observing what was taking place.
Light from above shone upon her brow with increasing brilliancy. Her eyes were still fixed; and,
to use earthly expressions, her chest began to
heave, her lips became motionless, and her glowing
countenance had the appearance of reverential
awe. Her looks were so expressive that I felt like
shrinking from her arms. I was so awed by her excitement that I did not notice its cause until, without turning her eyes, she raised up my head and
pointed in the direction indicated by her fixed attention.

To my utter astonishment, I there beheld the cause of her silent reverence and the wondrous admiration that pervaded the inhabitants of the city. There—oh, if the entire world only knew it!—there upon the cross, bleeding and dying, hung my Lord and Redeemer! Oh, that sight! No human heart can know its effects upon the spirits who wait in the infant paradise. The crown of thorns, the nails, the mangled form, the flowing blood, the look of compassion were so plainly manifested and combined that they conveyed to the soul an idea of the most intense and excruciating suffering.

Around the cross, congregating from every part of the city, were guardian angels with their infant spirits. As they gathered in a circle, all of them manifested deep humility and holy reverence. As soon as they had assumed this uniform attitude, they held out the infant spirits in their charge, directing their infant minds to the cross and the Sacrifice. At this moment an angel descended, clothed in bright garments, and moved around the cross, holding in his hand his glittering crown. Then, bowing, he worshipped, and his worship was as silent as that of all who had congregated. After this, turning to the guardian angels, he said, "Adore Him, for He is the Redeemer of a ruined race. Yes, let all heaven adore Him!"

The angel lifted up his right hand, and I saw in it a little book. In imitation, all the angels raised their right hands, each of which held a book of similar dimensions. Then appeared, as if from an invisible dome, a choir of angelic beings. These beings held palm branches in their hands, and with one voice they sang praises to God and the Lamb. They concluded by saying, *"'Let the little children come to Me...of such is the kingdom of heaven'* (Matt. 19:14). *'Out of the mouth of babes and nursing infants You have perfected praise'* (Matt. 21:16). Amen, alleluia, amen!"

Then the guardian angels drew still nearer to the cross, presenting the spirits in their charge, while they were addressed in a manner entirely beyond my comprehension. At the close of the address, each infant was touched with a stream of light. The infants smiled and bowed their heads, while holding up in their little clasped hands the image of the cross, which had been given to them by their guardians. Again they were folded in the arms of their protectors, and again the choir chanted a loud anthem, which, being echoed by the surrounding spirits, filled the city with holy melody. Then the cross and the Sacrifice disappeared, the angels returned to their abode, and the city was restored to its former appearance.

During this manifestation, my guide had not moved or uttered a word but appeared to enter into the spirit of the scene and to realize that something of absorbing interest had been presented.

At length I inquired, "Is there no part of heaven without the cross and the Sacrifice? Each scene moves around its manifestation. Each spirit reveres it with holy awe, and each hymn of praise utters the name of the Sacrifice."

She replied in almost a whisper, "The cross is always before the vision of redeemed spirits. In every circle the cross is seen. Every flower, every artistic production, has the cross worked throughout it, as if by an invisible hand. All instruction is based upon that blessed symbol of redeeming love, and it is the duty of the guardian angels to instruct the spirits in their charge concerning the great truth of redemption through Jesus, who suffered upon the cross.

"For this purpose, each class of spirits, as it passes from its first guardian protectors to the care of others, is congregated in a similar manner. By this means, the cross and the Sacrifice are etched upon the infant spirits' minds and hearts. The cross shines forth from the soul that has received its impression. But where the cross does not shine, there is no pure love, and the heart in which it is not visible is not at peace with God. Because of this, malicious spirits cannot conceal their real nature from angels or *'the spirits of just men made perfect'* (Heb. 12:23). In heaven there can be no guile.

"But, Marietta, this is only an introductory view of the principles that, in due time, will be more perfectly unfolded to you."

chapter 6

Scenes of Glory and Wretchedness

✤

At that moment, I heard a voice from above us saying, "Come up here." When I looked up, I saw a circular expanse winding upward into the superior glory. This was similar to the interior of a tower whose spiral walls form ascending platforms. This lovely pathway seemed to be formed of rainbows wrapped in spirals of prismatic hues and reflecting varying but ever beautiful tints of matchless luster.

Carried on a cloud of light that, like a chariot, gently ascended the spiral, we passed from the surface of the city and moved along the rising galleries of this rainbow tower. Seated by the side of my companion, the spirit who had kissed the cross, a sense of calm composure, holy peace, and superior delight captivated and pervaded my heart. The spiral gallery, which seemed to undulate as if moved by breath, became more beautiful as we went on. It appeared to be composed of minute gems of floating light, reflecting in their surfaces each floral beauty that had gladdened my eyes in the city from which I had just arisen.

I did not have time, however, to distinguish between the various qualities of luster and to define their loveliness. We soon emerged from the ascending gallery of rainbows and stood upon a high plain, resting in the transparent air above the magnificent dome that crowned the center temple of instruction.

From this position, I looked upon the great city extending on every side beneath my view. At a glance, I could see the general features of its plan, and I contemplated it in its entire form as a picture of surpassing loveliness.

Beneath me was the sublime temple of instruction, built of precious materials in a style of architecture that I am unable to describe. It arose from the center of an expansive circular lawn, whose green surface appeared to be covered with the softest and richest greenness. Majestic trees arose in groups and at regular intervals, bearing a profusion of fragrant and shining clusters of flowers. Beneath their shade, and on the more open spaces, appeared tiny flower beds, filled with every variety of flowers and blossoming shrubs and vines. Fountains of living waters were also visible. Some rose from the green grass and flowed through marble channels or through beds of golden sands with a low and pleasant murmur, while others gushed forth in full volume to a great height and descended in glowing streams of every variety of form. The waters of these latter fountains were received in basins, some of which were like diamonds, and others like burnished silver or the whitest pearl.

This lawn was encircled by lofty but open trelliswork. At its eastern side, a gateway without doors appeared. From the center of this gateway, a stream of living water flowed forth, supplied from the fountains within the enclosure.

I now directed my attention to the surrounding city and perceived that it was divided into twelve great sections by the river of living waters. This river, flowing in a spiral course, was bordered on either side by a wide avenue. I also perceived that twelve other streets intersected this spiral avenue, centering in the consecrated ground around the temple and radiating to twelve equally divided points at the outer limit of the scene.

As my vision followed the pathway of the flowing river and the stately avenues, my mind became absorbed in the entrancing sight. The city was divided into one hundred and forty-four great wards, arranged in a series of advancing degrees of prestige and beauty. From the outer limit to the center was one gently ascending and encircling pathway of ever increasing loveliness. Each degree was marked by new and more beautiful forms of trees, flowers, fountains, statues, palaces, and temples of adoration. Each building was of vast extent and corresponded with all others as the perfect part of a most perfect whole.

In this way, the entire city appeared to be one garden of flowers, one grove of foliage, one gallery of sculptured imagery, one undulating sea of fountains, one unbroken extent of magnificent architecture— all set in a surrounding landscape of corresponding beauty. Above was a sky adorned with hues of immortal light that bathed and encircled each and every object with an ever varying and increasing charm.

I now saw the movement of the inhabitants. But I can give only a faint idea of what was moving before my sight. I can only describe their movement by saying that it was all melody. The angelic multitudes appeared to be animated by one inspiring Love. They moved in the wisdom of one orderly plan, and their intention was to place their infant charges into conditions that would perfectly correspond to all the visible perfection. No angel's movement was disconnected from the universal harmony. Rather, all appeared to cooperate and to be inspired from one superior Source.

I saw that no rivalry or desire of selfish glory existed in the lovely groups of infants. Instead, the inhabitants of each nursery were united in holy affection to the superior, associated, and more mature societies. Each little child was filled with holy love and desired to become advanced in holy wisdom and be prepared to be used as a vessel of light and loveliness. I also saw that each delighted to learn from those above; each found joy in communicating beautiful forms, as gifts of holy love and wisdom, to those below, and in exercising the entire being in harmonious and unselfish works of love.

In this it was revealed that each child and each group of children advanced in orderly progression from temple to temple, from palace to palace, and from circle to circle. As one group advanced, it occupied the place just vacated by an older group, and in its former abode gave place to a more youthful family. Thus, like the movement of spring upon some unfallen paradise, I saw each little child unfold from beauty to beauty like a living blossom of immortality. Meanwhile, everything above them was glory, everything around them was loveliness, and everything within them was harmonious movement of unfolding life, love, knowledge of heaven, adoration of the Savior, and inspiration of undying joy.

Having thus beheld the city of infant paradise in its glory, usefulness, and magnificence, my vision expanded. Beyond the circle of palaces, I saw more perfectly what I had seen before while in the city: multitudes of angels gathered around in readiness to enter the outer temples at the appointed time. Each group was congregating according to the school to which the infants who were with them belonged.

These angels approached as on wings of wind. Around them, enrobing them, was a bright cloud that made them appear as if they were clothed with the sun. Still in their arms were infant spirits whose existence appeared to depend upon their care.

As they drew very near, each guardian angel would pause a moment, hovering in the holy and serene atmosphere. Then, inclining to an appropriate position, the angel would rest.

The delightful unfolding of this glorious view was now somewhat changed. My guide therefore addressed me, saying, "Marietta, behold the order and glorious wonders of the first and simplest degree of spiritual paradise. These angels you have seen are ever engaged in their delightful employment. Here, as you have been taught, infants assemble from the earthly world. From this blessed realm, they are conducted to other, higher schools of instruction. But before you are permitted to advance, a solemn and instructive lesson will be given to you."

Despairing Thoughts

My guide touched my forehead again, and the brightness and glory of the scene departed. I immediately descended and soon was in a low and gloomy subterraneous vault. Thick folds of darkness encompassed me, and a feeling of supernatural dread entered my soul and shocked my being. My spirit shrank back at every movement of my mind. Indeed, it appeared as if my thoughts wrestled amid the darkness. A distant roar broke upon my ears, as if an ocean's mighty waters were foaming and surging down some rough, rocky waterfall. In vain I sought to grasp something by which I might slow my rapid movement toward the awful abyss.

At this moment a blue flash disturbed the vault of darkness below. As the light disappeared, all around me floated grim phantoms, each enveloped in the fire of unhallowed passion. So sudden had been the change, and so dreadful its effects upon me, that no thought but those of horror and despair had entered my mind until these gruesome ghosts appeared. A more fearful terror now possessed me, and I turned to seek refuge in the embrace of my guide. But, alas! I did not find her! Alone and in this dreadful place, I was left with no way to express the faintest idea of the agony of that moment.

At first I thought I would pray, but in an instant, the whole scene of my life was before me. Then I exclaimed, "Oh, for one short hour on earth! Oh, for time, however brief, to prepare my soul and to ensure that I am fit for the world of spirits!" But my conscience, as if it were some fiend, echoed in a hoarse and trembling voice, "In your day you rejected and spurned the means adapted to your sinful condition. How can you hope for successful petition in this dark scene of woe?" And then, to add to my misery, my former doubts and skepticism arose like living beings, looking upon me with piercing glares. They revolved around me in condemning mockery, as though each was a self-actuated body. Thus congregated my life's meditations. All my secret thoughts now composed a part of that attending multitude; even the thoughts I had forgotten now proceeded in order and strength around me.

To escape them was to flee from my own life. To annihilate them would seem to blot out my own existence. I realized the force of the Savior's expression, *"For every idle word men may speak, they will give account of it in the day of judgment"* (Matt. 12:36).

While my mind was thus pondering the outward vision of my despairing thoughts, and while in absolute wretchedness my spirit longed to be delivered from the gloom below and to repossess the bodily form it once had, another terrible scene was suddenly made visible. It was the full and perfect representation of my crucified Redeemer.

Suddenly, and in one continuous vision, my entire thought-life concerning Him passed in separate embodiments before my mind. In one compartment of vision, dotted with appropriate imagery, appeared those thoughts that I had had of Him as a man. In another compartment, also in corresponding images, appeared a representation of my thoughts in which I had pictured Him as divine. In still another compartment appeared a representation of my thoughts concerning His special atonement for the elect. There, in fearful forms, appeared those thoughts that had been mine when I had imagined myself to be predestined to reprobation from eternity and therefore doomed to endless punishment.

Other compartments appeared, also with appropriate forms. One contained my thoughts concerning an eternal salvation of mankind that does not require special moral reformation or a personal and living faith in the Savior's atoning sacrifice. Another contained thoughts concerning salvation by works, ignoring the need for a special inward faith in divine grace. These separate compartments blended in one revolving sphere around me, in which ten thousand confused images were rapidly combining and separating. They at once bewildered, excited, and overwhelmed my mind.

Thus, my mental being moved in fearful vision around my thoughts. Every phase of doctrine concerning Christ, heaven, hell, religion, or eternal life that I had ever heard or studied comprised part of the tremendous sight.

Oh, how bewildering were these conflicting yet associated ideas of the Redeemer! As they encircled me in one confused yet coherent cloud of imagery, I saw in each some distorted view of the Savior. From none of them could I behold Him as He is. Therefore, His divine glory, honor, majesty, and perfection could not be manifested in their exalting and redeeming power, and I could not see Him as a Prince and a Savior in the true character that He upholds to the world.

chapter 7

A Solemn Lesson

❧

I was bewildered and ready to abandon all hope of ever escaping that horrible abyss. I had determined in my mind that this sight would be the last to fill the cup of woe from which I had already drunk to agony and that could not be drained for all eternity. But suddenly I saw the Savior extending His arms toward me, while from His lips fell the lovely and soul-enrapturing sentence, *"Come to Me, all you who labor and are heavy laden, and I will give you rest"* (Matt. 11:28).

How vast the contrast when that glorious Being, encompassed with the shining appearance of the sun, was revealed from the midst of the cloud! In the revolving halo of light that encircled Him, I beheld a representation of the true relationship between the divine Redeemer and the universe of light, where holy angels dwell. There appeared an awful disparity between my own nature and that sphere of light, life, harmony, and love.

I thus beheld Him whom, in my foolishness and skepticism, I had so often rejected. At first I wished to break from the mental embodiment that was around my inner being, to mingle the very elements of my life with this sphere of light, and to dwell in its beauty, peace, and joy. But because of the diversity existing between its intrinsic nature and the impure elements of my fallen mind, I was unable to enter into its reality; and so a feeling of distrust and doubt again arose within me.

The Phantom Sphere

Suddenly a black veil of night appeared to ascend, pervading and encompassing my being. My inner doubt seemed to be like a cloud that shut out the light of the upper glory, and a spirit of denial plunged me into the vortex of a deeper gloom. I fell like one thrown from some dizzying height. The darkness opened to receive me. The moving shadow of a desolate abyss arose like clouds in dense masses of tempestuous gloom, and as I descended, the ever accumulating weight of darkness pressed more fearfully upon me.

At length, a lower plain that seemed boundless was projected upon my vision. At a little distance, it appeared to shine like metallic ores and to be covered with the sparkling semblance of vegetation. Waving trees with resplendent foliage, as well as flowers and fruits of crystal and gold, were visible in every direction.

Multitudes of spirits appeared beneath the foliage, and radiant garments were folded about each rapidly moving form. Some wore crowns upon their heads; others, tiaras; and others, decorations that appeared to be made of clusters of jewels, wreaths of golden coin, and cloth of gold and silver. Still others wore towering helmets; others wore circlets filled with glistening and waving plumes. A pale and flickering phosphorescence was emitted by every object, and all appeared as a splendid masquerade.

A Solemn Lesson

The apparel worn by these busy myriads corresponded with the ornaments on their heads; hence, every variety of luxurious apparel was displayed upon their bodies. Kings and queens appeared arrayed in the gorgeous robes of coronation. Groups of nobility, also decorated with all the varieties of adornment, displayed themselves in the pageantry of kingly courts. Dense multitudes were visible in garments peculiar to highly advanced nations. I discovered similar groups, composed of less civilized tribes, who were attired in barbaric ornaments of every form. While some appeared clothed in the garments of the present day, others were in ancient attire. In the midst of all this variety, every class of spirits manifested a uniformity of external pride, pomp, and rapidly moving and dazzling luster.

Sounds of mingled importance—bursts of laughter; utterances of revelry, lighthearted sport, witty ridicule, and polished sarcasm; obscene allusions; and terrible curses—broke upon my ears. These were intermixed with impure solicitations and backbitings, hollow compliments, and false congratulations. All in one fiery brilliancy, they agitated my already pained and bewildered senses.

As I advanced, I seemed to be walking on scorpions and treading amid living embers. The trees that seemed to wave about me were exhalations of fire, and their blossoms were the sparks and the burnings of incessant flames. Each object I approached created agony on contact.

The phosphorescent glare that surrounded the various objects burned the eyes that looked upon them. The fruit burned the hand that plucked and the lips that received it. The gathered flowers emitted a fiery breath, whose fetid and offensive odor caused excruciating pain when inhaled in the nostrils. The fiery atoms of the atmosphere burned as they wafted past me. The air and the blast that moved it were both burdened with disappointment and wretchedness.

When I turned to see if I could discover a single drop of water to relieve my fierce and intolerable thirst, fountains appeared, and water flowed in tiny streams amid the vegetation and lay in calm and placid pools. However, I soon discovered that these bodies of water corresponded with the former illusions, and the spray from the sparkling fountains fell like drops of molten lead upon the shrinking form. The flowing streams were like a molten river of metallic fire that flows from a furnace heated seven times beyond normal. And the deep, still pools were like white and waveless silver in some glowing crucible, when every atom is burning with a fierce, intolerable glow.

Suffering Revealed

While I was in solemn contemplation of these fearful scenes, a spirit approached me whom I had known on earth. This being appeared externally far more brilliant than it had appeared in the body. The form, the countenance, the eyes, and the hands appeared full of a metallic luster that varied with every motion and every thought.

Addressing me, the spirit said, "Marietta, we meet again. You see me as a disembodied spirit in the place where those who inwardly deny the Savior find their home when their mortal days have ended.

A Solemn Lesson

Strange emotions agitate your heart. I, too, felt the same sad and bewildered anxiety when I discovered this theater of my present existence. But I experienced what you have never yet realized in your mind.

"My life on earth was suddenly brought to a close, and as I departed from the world, I moved rapidly in the direction prompted by my ruling desires. I inwardly desired to be flattered, honored, and admired. I wanted to receive universal adulation and to be free to follow the perverted inclinations of my proud, rebellious, and pleasure-loving heart. I hoped for a state of existence where all would be pleasure without restraint, where each being would be free to obey the promptings of every passion, and where every indulgence would be permitted to the soul. I wanted to find a place where prayers and instructions would have no place, where the Sabbath would not be known, where no rebuke of sin would ever fall, and where existence would be spent in lighthearted and festive sports, with no superior, restraining power to disturb or interfere.

"With these desires, I entered the spirit world and passed to the condition adapted to my inward state. I rushed to the enjoyment of the glittering scenes that you now behold. I was welcomed as you have not been, for at once I was recognized as a fitting associate by those who abide here. They do not welcome you, for they discern in you an inward desire that is opposed to the ruling passions that prevail here.

"I was welcomed with lighthearted and frolicsome sounds. The beings whom you behold in the distance rushed forward to embrace me. They shouted, 'Welcome! Welcome!' I was awed, bewildered, and yet energized by the atmosphere of this abode. I found myself filled with the power of strange and restless motion. A flood of thoughts that had been latent within me burst forth and filled my mind.

"Every organ and every pore of my being emitted a phosphorescent illumination that formed the appearance of a brilliant crown and reflected a wild, unearthly glow on the face. As it extended, the exhalation became a flaming robe that enveloped my form and caused me to appear like the other spirits associated with me.

"I became conscious of a strange sensation permeating my brain. A foreign power seemed to operate through it by an absolute possession.

"I abandoned myself to the attractive influences that were around me, and I sought to satisfy my desires for pleasure. I reveled, I banqueted, I mingled in the wild and voluptuous dance, I plucked the shining fruit, I plunged into the fiery streams, I glutted my nature with whatever appeared delicious and inviting to the senses. But when tasted, all was loathing and a source of increasing pain.

"The desires that are perpetuated here are so unnatural that what I crave I loathe and what delights tortures me. My torment creates within me a strange intoxication. My appetite is satiated, yet at the same time, my hunger is unappeased and unappeasable.

"Every object that I see, I crave; and I grasp it in the midst of disappointment and gather it with increased agony. With every new experience, I am immersed in some unknown fantasy, delirium, and intoxication. New and strange phenomena are continually manifested and add delirium to delirium, and fear to fear. I seem to have become part of what is around me, and the varied scenes that are mirrored upon the vision appear to radiate from me in a thousand constantly changing deceptions. The voices that fall on my ears burst from me in uncontrollable utterances. I laugh, philosophize, jeer, blaspheme, and ridicule by turns; yet every epithet, however impure, sparkles with wit, glows with metaphor, and is adorned with every rhetorical embellishment.

"The metallic ores, the waving trees, the shining fruit, the moving phantoms, and the deluding waters seem to form a dazzling and mocking spectacle that is ever before my eyes. Every subject of reflection has its equal in my heart. I inwardly long to satisfy my hunger and my thirst, and the desire appears to create around me a tantalizing illusion of cool waters I may never drink, grateful fruits I may never taste, refreshing breezes I may never feel, and peaceful slumbers I may never enjoy. I know that the forms around me are fantastic and delusive, yet every object appears to hold controlling power and to domineer with cruel enchantment over my bewildered mind.

"I am the slave of discordant and deceptive elements and of their presiding vices. By turns, every object attracts me. The thought of having a free mind dies with my dying will, and the idea that I am a part and an element of the revolving fantasy takes possession of my spirit.

"This realm, curtained with a cloud of night, is one sea of perversion and disease. Here lust, pride, hate, avarice, self-love, ambition, contention, and blasphemies revel in madness and kindle into a burning flame. And the kind of evil that does not belong to one spirit belongs to another, so that the combined strength of all the evil is the prevailing law. By this I am bound, and in it I exist.

"Here are those who oppressed the poor, robbed the employee of his wages, and bound the weary with heavy burdens. Here are the false in religious faith, the hypocrites, the adulterers, the assassin, and the suicide who, not satisfied with life in the external form, hurried its end.

"If mortals only knew the dark and dreadful night into which they are sure to fall if they die unprepared, they would desire to lengthen the time of testing rather than to speed its termination—no matter how heavy their sorrow might be. They would wish to wisely improve the fleeting moments of trial on the earth. Man's weary existence is laden with grief while he walks the gloomy valleys of death and gropes along the thorny paths that mortals tread. But here, new and multiplied causes of accumulating gloom awake on all sides. The hope of peaceful and happy days in the outer world flickers like the dying flame. In this abode are ceaseless, unsatisfied, and unholy inclinations.

"Here in this place, the senses are infinitely more acute. What would produce only a pang with mortals enters into the very elements of our existence, and the pain becomes a part of us. The consciousness and capacity of suffering here are far superior to those of human suffering.

"Marietta, I feel it is futile to attempt to describe our deplorable state. I often inquire, 'Is there no hope?' And my intellect replies, 'How can there be hope? How can harmony exist in the very midst of discord?' We were warned of the consequences of our course while in the body, but we loved our ways better than those that exalted the soul. We have fallen into this fearful abode. We have brought about our own sorrow. God is just. He is good. We know that we do not suffer from a vindictive law of our Creator. Our violation of the moral law, by which our moral natures should have been preserved in harmony and health, is the prime cause of our state. O sin, you parent of countless woes! You insidious enemy of peace and heaven! Why do mortals love your ways?"

Here she paused and focused her eyes, wild with despair, upon me. I shrank from the dreadful, piercing look, for her appearance manifested inexpressible torture.

A Vital Warning

While she was addressing me, a multitude of the forlorn beings were moving around her, striving to suppress their true feelings while listening to her tell the reality of their sufferings. Their appearance, her address, and the scene that was before me filled me with horror, and I sought to escape. When she saw that I desired to flee, her grief appeared to deepen, and she hastily said, "No, Marietta, do not leave me. Can you not endure for a short period the sight and story of what I am continually suffering? Tarry with me, for I desire to speak of many things.

"Do you shrink back at these scenes? Know, then, that all that moves around you is only the outer degree of deeper woe. Marietta, no good and happy being abides with us. Everything within is dark. We sometimes dare to hope for redemption, still remembering the story of redeeming love, and inquire, 'Can that love penetrate this abode of gloom and death? May we ever hope to be made free from the desires and inclinations that bind us like chains and the passions that burn like consuming fires in the unholy elements of this world of wretchedness?'"

Overcome by her deep feelings, she then yielded to the expression of grief, and I heard her speak no more.

Just then, another spirit drew near. Addressing me, this spirit said, "Go, leave us to our lot. Your presence gives us pain, since it revives active memories of lost opportunities."

Here the spirit paused a moment, then continued, "No, wait. Prompted by a cause unknown to me, I want you to hear what we have learned here about the power and influence of evil on the spirit of man. Though evil is exceedingly subtle while man inhabits the body of clay, it forms the external sphere of his existence when his spirit leaves the outer world and enters the spiritual world. Here where we abide, evil is our outward dwelling. It arises from the deep. It unfolds from the soul. It encompasses all, pervades all, controls and inspires all.

"Mortals are opposed to this truth. From the love and goodness of God, they reason that there cannot be suffering in the spiritual realm. But this kind of reasoning must conclude that God also desires evil, since evil and suffering exist with mankind in the outer world and also prevail with us. The cause of this is obvious, and yet men seek to reject the principle.

A Solemn Lesson

"When man disturbs or prevents the harmony of God's law, evil consequences ensue, and man produces an effect contrary to what was prescribed for him. Therefore, what was intended to lead to life, what should have perfected him, now leads to death. Thus, sin, or the violation of God's law, disqualifies him from proper development. Being removed from harmony, the violator ceases to exist in the law of peace and holy development. This great and irrevocable truth is seen every time that God's laws are opposed.

"Why will mortals not use reason and recognize the results of their actions? By preventing the growth of evil and by cleaving to God, through heaven-appointed means, they would escape these fearful consequences. Marietta, you are not one of us, or else these elements would have enveloped your being and absorbed your life already. But you will return to realms of peace. Madness and delirium arise and rage within us upon hearing of places where love, pure love, and peace abide. You are thus addressed because of your return to earth. Tell the inhabitants of earth what you have seen, and warn them of the danger awaiting those who persist in the gratification of impure desires."

One hideous expression closed the scene as I was removed from it. I was overcome by what I had seen, knowing that it was so real. I had known those spirits on earth, and when I saw them there, I knew them still. But how changed! They were now the very embodiment of sorrow and remorse. How ardently I desired that they might escape, become pure, and receive an inheritance with those blessed spirits I had visited in the paradise of peace!

chapter 8

Address of the False
Philosopher

❧

During these reflections, I unconsciously passed from that sphere of gloom to a region where I could perceive nothing but lonely space. No sun or stars were visible to my sight. Dense darkness closed around me, and I felt that my doom was sealed and that I would soon become the companion of spirits in those fantastic realms. When I began to agonize beneath the idea of departing hope, I heard a voice from the distance say, in tones soft and melodious, "Look unto Jesus; He is the life of the soul."

A feeling immediately arose within me in rebellion to the idea of adoring Jesus who was crucified. But suddenly, all that seemed to sustain me departed, and again I descended as from an immeasurable height into an abyss inhabited by beings more desperate than those from whom I had just escaped. They gathered around me and commended me for the doubt I had entertained concerning the divinity of the Son of God.

Then a spirit of great intellect approached me and said, "Religion, the religion of the Bible, so much revered by many who live in darkness and are undeveloped, is but a spiritual farce. The God of the Bible, whom Christians call the Savior of the world,

was only a man. Religious faith limits the range of
human thought, fetters the noble intellect, and prevents the progression of the race. Those you have
just visited are a group of spirits who, blinded by the
delusive dreams of earth's religionists, have entered
the spirit world without having progressed. Hence,
they still cling to the idea of redemption through
Christ. They appear to suffer, but their suffering is
imaginary.

"Before long, light will reach them. Then they
will discover the foolishness of their religious education, to which they cleave with insatiable desire,
though they discarded it with their better beings. We
are free. Our intellects roam unrestrained, and we
behold the magnificence and the glory of the peopled
universe. We enjoy the rich productions of the mind.
In this way—not by the religion of the cross—we
arise into the more exalted spheres of intellectual
attainments and the moving grandeur of terrestrial
things.

"Marietta, we saw you when darkness overshadowed you. We understood that, because of the way
you were educated, you would have offered prayer
for salvation in the name of Jesus. We heard the
voice that spoke from above you, saying, 'Look to
Jesus.' That voice did not save you. Learn, then, that
salvation comes from the natural progress of your
being and your mind.

"What do you see, Marietta? Abandon your
thoughts of the empty religion of the Bible, and behold the wonders of this sphere of existence. Around
you gather minds from the varied spheres of earth,
minds whose intellectual strength could not yield to
the force of an imaginary religion. They were not

awed into reverence by the priestly garb, nor did they sing the idle notes of psalmody, the heartless 'music' of the church.

"Instead, these minds sing of nature, of which they are a noble part. Thus united, they ascend the octave of progressive harmony of the mind."

Just then the spirit addressing me became greatly annoyed, and the nebulous appearance that encompassed him was agitated by successive shocks, which caused his whole being to convulse and writhe beneath its influence. I could not perceive their origin, and I was greatly terrified. The whole scene changed at every successive shock, which was accompanied by flashes of pale light playing upon the cloudlike form that enveloped him.

I could also perceive that he was intensely struggling to overcome some power that was about to control him. All of his energy was exerted to its highest capacity to roll back the tide that was overwhelming him. Suddenly he groaned with the bitterness of one sinking into irremediable despair, and then he yielded to the intrusive influence.

A vast arena then opened to my view, in which I saw at one glance every imaginable kind of vice, human society, government, organization, and all the varied phases and forms of worship in every kind of religion. I saw everyone from the heathen to the fashionable churchgoing people who heartlessly worship under the name of the holy religion of the cross.

chapter 9

The Pandemonium of Mock Worship

❧

As this scene opened, I heard a voice from far above me, saying, "Marietta, do not fear. Here you see a pandemonium where the self-deceived congregate, along with hopers in false philosophy, together with the despisers of God. The false religions of earth also arise here in supernatural form, hypocrisy unveils its hideous shape, and religious mockery speaks in its own language. Human wolves, who appeared in sheep's clothing, are exhibited here so that they might indulge their avarice upon the humble and unsuspecting. Listen! Hear the wild chant that breaks from the thousands who sit in the galleries of song. They once sang— heartlessly sang—hymns dedicated to the worship of the living God. Listen to the hoarse voice of the heavy organ before which they are congregated. Watch them arise, observe their manner, and seek to understand what they are saying."

No one can ever know the reality of such a scene, except those who personally behold it. I am only able to say that every evil scheme that prevails with man appeared to be organized and moving perfectly in this scene. Each spirit was an actor performing the part that he had cultivated while in the body. All of them struggled in vain to obtain enjoyment, which, from its dreadful fantasy, recoiled upon the suffering soul with inexpressible horror.

As I looked upon them, the occupants of the broad galleries arose and began to sing. As they sang, the hoarse voice of the organ jarred, as note after note of their attempted music fell from lips whose very accents mocked the effort. My soul pitied them as I saw them sink back in utter despair, yet I thought I could perceive some purpose in their movements.

An Unholy Minister

Below this choir was seated a disdainful audience. Before the audience and behind a pulpit of Gothic architecture stood a man clad in priestly garb—one who had dishonored the cause of the Redeemer by hypocrisy, vanity, and pride; one who had made the cause of the holy ministry a common thing by his soulless profession of love for the gifts of grace.

This speculator in religious things moved in the mock dignity of his occupation. Before him lay an open volume, from which he attempted to read, but every effort to do so was baffled. His voice was shrill and piercing, his accents inarticulate. His features became distorted; he writhed and agonized. He then attempted to read again, but the attempt ended the same way, only increasing his sufferings. He burst forth in the most vehement expressions, cursing his own being and everyone around him, and then blasphemously addressed himself to the Author of existence. He charged God with all wrong, with being the source of every sorrow, and he even desired to gather together the strength of all created intellects so that he might curse the Creator of the universe.

His cursing, his manner, and his insatiable passion caused him to appear so desperate that I feared that he had power to accomplish great destruction in whatever direction he moved.

Soon, however, my anxiety was relieved by the sudden exhaustion of his entire force. I saw that he was limited in power and was, to a very great extent, under the will of his audience.

One glance at the crowd before him was sufficient to reveal the cause of much of his suffering. Seated there were those whose countenances spoke of inward hate mingled with wild, raving enjoyment. They mocked his futile efforts and indulged in fiendish delight at the expense of his dreadful sufferings. Indeed, they relished his keen manifestation of despair.

As the priest sank back, the expression of his face was that of horror beyond description. His being assumed every imaginable distortion. Around him flashed dim fires, and his entire outward expression revealed an inward consciousness as restless as some burning crater. His whole appearance spoke of agonies equal to the worst ideas of the relentless sinner's hell, and it reminded me of the words of Jesus when He said, "[These] *will be cast out into outer darkness. There will be weeping and gnashing of teeth*" (Matt. 8:12). I was also reminded that "*their worm does not die, and the fire is not quenched*" (Mark 9:44).

His Listeners Respond

While this minister lay enveloped in the fires of his own unholy passions, a member of his audience arose and thus addressed him: "You fiend of darkness! You child of hypocrisy! Deceiver, matchless deceiver! Yours is the hell of a heartless religious teacher. You can never endure adequate sufferings. You turned religion and the souls of men into merchandise to be bought and sold. Indeed, because of this, you dwelled in temples of human glory, receiving the adoration of men. Then you wrapped yourself in the garments of ease at the expense of others' souls; you did not seek to reach the ruined heart with the soul-redeeming truth of heaven, but rather to please the ears and charm the imagination.

"Now you are tormented. Arise, you false teacher! Arise, and in your silken gown display the order of your false apostleship. Speak smooth things to us. Direct the movement of this broad gallery of mimicked song. Hold your blasphemy! Do not vent your curses, for your Maker is just; do not wish to remove Him from His throne. You have mocked His supreme majesty. Through you, His glory should have been shown, and by that light thousands should have been led to seek His face."

At this sharp rebuke, the suffering priest sought to escape. The speaker therefore continued, "No, you hypocrite! Even though you want to, you cannot flee. Look over this vast throng of sufferers, then ask yourself what is the cause of our suffering. Though these have sinned, and though each stands or falls before his Master, can you behold them in peace and with a sense of innocence? Did you strive to lead them to God? No, you did not. Instead, your elaborate expositions of the sacred Word, adorned with poetic genius and addressed most eloquently, only served to lead the dormant spirit into deeper slumber, while you decorated your mortal brow with human praise."

The Agony of Regret

Here the minister cried out, "Spare me! Spare me! I suffer the tortures of unabating remorse! Dreaded retribution, delay your assault! Do not cut your victim down! I acknowledge that my sufferings are just. In earthly life I sought means of human pleasure. I trifled with the souls of men and heartlessly wrote of eternal things. I formed my prayers for human hearing and interpreted the sacred Scriptures to gratify the capricious, the selfish, the braggart in holy things, the usurper of human rights, the oppressor.

"Oh, horror! The horrors of immortal night and keen remorse take hold of my spirit. I hear the voice of lamentation. I see the madness of disappointed spirits. These haunt me. If I seek to flee, I am surrounded by the multitude of ills hanging upon the souls that find no rest here. These, my parishioners, drive me mad with their bitter curses. Secret sins, like demons commissioned to inflict immortal pain on me, arise from the vault of my memory. Spare me a deeper hell!"

Sin's Consequences

During these exclamations, the whole audience arose and mocked his agony. When the minister had finished, the spirit addressing him resumed his hostile criticism, saying, "You knew very well that our delight was to please you. When we indulged in the gratification of unholy desires that led us in the ways of death, you, our religious teacher, administered no reproof. The Bible—oh, that sacred Book, gift of God to guide the wanderer to bright mansions in heaven—was made, by the false interpretations of the pleasure-loving and heartless minister, our passport to this place of woe. Here, sins ripen into living forms. Here, fashionable clothes, with their gaudy folds, enwrap the spirit with innumerable sheets of inextinguishable fire. And here, mammon, like a supernatural goddess, sits in the clouds of death that form a canopy over the abyss below.

"When the laws of life are inverted, the result is the fantasy in which you are now moving. You have done this, urged on by the love of glory—the glory of the hypocrites, whose form of religion makes them like *'whitewashed tombs'* (Matt. 23:27). Outwardly, your heart is as spotless as the church that reflects the glory of the spiritual Jerusalem from bright worlds on high. But this same heart was the seat of pride and lust, a cage of foul birds, a den of treacherous thoughts. (See Revelation 18:2.) Yes, it was a tomb *'full of dead men's bones'* (Matt. 23:27), the fragments of departed, heartless ministers, the legacy of religious bigots.

"Do not curse your Maker. This is your just reward. Listen to the Scriptures that often fell from your lips so carelessly: *'For he who sows to his flesh will of the flesh reap corruption'* (Gal. 6:8); *'The wages of sin is death'* (Rom. 6:23). How those passages of Holy Writ resound in the chambers of souls congregated in the realms of night! They touch every immortal sensation that has been drawn to its highest tension by the horror of the scenes that arise like ghosts from beneath these spheres of death.

"No, false teacher, let God be true, for sin has formed us this way. We suffer the consequences of violated law, the law of our beings."

As these words were spoken, a fearful trembling seized the form of the one who had risen in the audience. He became more and more agitated, until he shook and fell like a dead man. The congregation trembled and fell with him. Losing identity, they looked like one vast body of agitated life. Above this body arose a thick atmosphere of moving atoms, a cloud so dense that it resembled a part of the mass below.

The sight was too much for me. Being unable to endure further these scenes of woe, I shrank back and exclaimed, "Is there not a God of mercy? Can He look on and not save these people?"

"Yes," spoke a voice from above me. "Yes, there is a God of mercy, and that God looks on sinners with pity. Have you not read, *'God so loved the world that He gave His only begotten Son, that whoever believes in Him should not perish but have everlasting life'* (John 3:16)? However, though salvation is offered to the world, and though heaven's messengers plead with the sinner, millions refuse. Millions more who claim to be followers of God are only taking a chance with the great truth connected with man's redemption. When sin is indulged in, it prepares the sinner for woe, and there are many who will not forsake their evil ways until they have fallen into the most wretched state—the consequence of their violation of the laws of purity and love.

"Fear not, Marietta. Before your eyes has been portrayed part of the consequences of sin upon the spirit of man. Spiritual sufferings are beyond any power of expression; they cannot be perfectly mirrored upon the understanding by representative illustrations. The false philosopher who first addressed you represents the spirit of antichrist that seeks to dazzle spiritual perception with bright pictures of false reasoning. Behind all of his intellectualism lies discord, improper affections, impure desires, self-love, a false heart, cruelty, lust, devastation, murder, sacrilege, blasphemy, and the denial of God in His redeeming mercy. He strove to direct your attention to an opposite scene in order to conceal the state of those whose hearts are not controlled by the love of God.

"The fact that his power failed represents the utter inability of all things outside of Christ to save the soul from the influences that, through sin, infect the unregenerate heart and lead to death.

"Then you saw a scene in which all forms of vice were likewise portrayed, though it would have weighed too heavily upon you if you had seen this view displayed in all its fullness. Consequently, there immediately appeared the gallery of choristers. These represent the world making melody to the gods of their worship, of whatever name or character they happened to be. Their hearts held no fear or love of the Supreme Being whom they mocked with lip service. In the pulpit, a false teacher and the awful consequences of hypocrisy in religion were portrayed. He was false and had therefore fallen into this pit of woe. Before him were those who represent people who worship in the name of the cross, but who do not have the fear of God. To all appearances, they seemed to worship God, but their hearts were far from Him (Isa. 29:13). They sought to please themselves in their devotions, while they chose a teacher who in turn sought to glorify himself with men by gratifying the caprice of his audience.

"This minister strove to address his audience concerning this great truth: that the mind works out in the spirit the impressions received in the outer world. His ineffective effort represented the inability of any being to derive real satisfaction, or to be useful to those around him, by false methods.

"The spirit who addressed him from the audience represents those who trusted false teachers and had little concern for their own spiritual condition. The members of this particular audience charged their sins upon each other. Thus, you witnessed the discord of beings who are not properly united. When the spirit referred to the justice of their condition as a natural consequence following the violation of law, he was representing the consciousness of guilt and of the goodness of God—the consciousness that is in all who awake from their idle dreaming to a proper sense of the demands of God's holy law upon them.

"You witnessed the dreadful writhing of the spirit addressed under the dark picture of his past deeds. This told you that when those who follow their carnal desires in the external life meet in spirit, they reflect great truths upon each other by their thoughts and movements. Their final fall and blending into one illustrates the inseparable nature and tendency of sin. The law of sympathy exists even with the disembodied spirits of men, and by that law, they are attracted to each other and heap more and more sorrow upon each other. The moving cloud above them also illustrates the atmosphere of thought that fills the great arena of spiritual discord.

"Finally, Marietta, the scene of the bishop and his congregation, together with the false teachers of the schools of vain philosophy, illustrates the portion of the Scriptures that says, *'If the blind leads the blind, both will fall into a ditch'* (Matt. 15:14). Marietta, your spirit cannot endure more. Let this lesson impress you with the great truth that *'the wages of sin is death'* (Rom. 6:23)."

chapter 10

A Sphere of Harmony

⚜

A s the voice addressing me ceased, I heard an angel say, "Marietta, come up here!" I arose into a cloud of light that gently ascended. My spirit rested in its refuge.

The change—how great, how marvelous! A moment before, I was with fear and wonder beholding a suffering throng reveling in the madness of inflamed passions—passions cultivated to excessive indulgence while in the body. These beings were filled with sorrow; the undisguised effects of evil of every kind were manifested in them: demoralizing habits, secret purposes, hidden iniquity, and so on. There were contentions, murmurings, and dreadful blasphemies, while the sufferers and those who had caused their suffering were drawn together and held by prevailing elements—the elements of their own perverted natures.

From their condition, I learned that sin brings death and that happiness does not come by disobedience but by unsophisticated religious faith—faith in Jesus as the Redeemer—that stirs up the true worship of God from a broken heart and contrite spirit. (See Psalm 34:18.) I also learned that deceit was the element of darkness and the source of many woes, as well as the concealing shelter of the results of falsehood and the fruits of vice. Yet plainly revealed was the great truth that no deception, however finely performed, can hide in the hour of trial. Even he who attempted to portray the glories of nature, who sought to lure the soul from the cross, and who endeavored to offer life and peace by other means, failed to conceal the drama moving in the broad arena where those who neither love God nor regard His law congregate.

I was reflecting upon this scene when new light broke in upon me. I turned to see its source, when above me I saw a lovely being clad in garments bright as the sun, resting in the glory surrounding her. Her face shone with heavenly goodness. She dwelt calmly in the midst of the divine brilliance. She spoke in a voice that filled me with delight, saying, "Rest, spirit; rest. Let no care weary you. Dismiss your thoughts of the scenes just passed. God has prepared a mansion in heaven for every willing heart, and whoever seeks will find the Lord a present help in time of need (Ps. 46:1). Those you have seen are in the element they indulged while in the body. Just as he who falls from some dizzy height must bear the pain imparted by the wound, so he who lives and dies in sin receives the reward of his sin. This is the law of being.

"Rest, Marietta; rest. Listen to the bands of angels who descend. That harmony, how sweet! How gently it moves along the heavenly way! It nears us, Marietta; the volume swells upon the heavenly breeze. Its notes accent praises to our Redeemer. Heavenly anthems awake on every side. Look up, Marietta; we are near a city in which righteousness dwells. No evil enters there. No false spirit will ever pollute the holy temples thereof.

Hark, sister spirit, a guardian angel of the holy hills addresses you."

Then there came a voice saying, "Marietta, where are you? Have you left the world of mortal sadness? Why are you inclined to scenes where evil passions reign? Does your being vacillate between the spheres of good and evil? I saw you in the paradise of peace, moving with the blessed ones, where songs unite and anthems are ever ascending in softest melody. I saw you floating in the murky air, friendless and alone. I witnessed your sudden fall into the cloud that overhangs the arena of inharmonious, wicked beings. I saw you observing every movement until the sight overcame you. As you sank beneath the burdened vision, I heard you call for help from God or for some kind angel to befriend you.

"Learn from this, Marietta, that he whose heart is not established in truth, whose nature is not controlled by the law of holy love, is exposed to the attracting influence of evil, for there is no safety for the one not born of divine goodness. He who does not have this truth will be exposed to influences that lead to outer darkness and to the abode of death. Remember, he who wishes to be the disciple of Truth and enter into rest must deny himself the gratification of the unholy inclinations of the perverted heart; he must cleave to what inspires reverence for God and a desire to be found doing His will. He must convert the attributes of his being to the exercise of well-doing, for in this way, and only in this way, can he secure everlasting good through divine grace.

"Marietta, these scenes and the opening of your spiritual perceptions are permitted for a wise purpose.

87

You have represented the activity of human minds that are unsettled in religious truth. You were first attracted to paradise, then to vacant regions where Chaos and Night rule as chief monarchs, and then to scenes of wretchedness where abide those whose characters have been formed by indulging in wrongdoing. The latter cherished their wrongdoing, until their minds became drunk with the excess of vice and they became delirious under the influence of hallucinating pleasures. Thus it is revealed that, when left to itself, the perverted spirit drives madly on under the insatiable influence of evil.

"The spirits you saw in the broad arena only serve to aggravate each other's woe and are therefore mutual sufferers. It is the same in the mortal world: one evildoer supports another in the ways of evil. In this you see how *'one sinner destroys much good'* (Eccl. 9:18). Sin added to sin enlarges its capacity and increases its advancement, until families, tribes, and nations arm themselves to do battle on its behalf.

"Oh, that mortals only knew the power of evil's influence! Then, prompted by the law of heavenly love, which is the Spirit of grace, they would unite to prevent the workings of evil in the carnal heart. Marietta, the word *misery* may well be written across the race of man, for by their indulgence in sin, human beings embitter their mortal existence and too often enter the world of spirits inclining to evil. Then they become united to those existing where similar elements prevail. But the grace of God, if admitted into the understanding and emotions, changes the character and inclinations of man. Divine life descending into the soul turns the soul's inclinations toward the Source of that divine life. When such individuals enter here by the law of holy attraction, they mingle in life's sustaining sphere and receive from God the inspiration of holiness.

The Center Dome of Infant Paradise

"Marietta, this is the city where you have beheld the infant nurseries. From scenes of sorrow and death, you are permitted to return to this place. Here above the center dome of the infant nursery, you can look upon the order and function of this temple of education. The schools of infant paradise are congregated here, and here the infants are instructed in the higher degrees of useful employment."

As the spirit ceased to speak, suddenly the great dome below us opened and presented in one glance its glory and magnificence. In it I saw all the grandeur, variety, and order of the entire paradise. Again, I saw the cross in the center. Around it were twelve spirits, in each of whose hands was a smaller cross and a harp. Upon their heads were crowns bright with gems. Below these, and filling the broad arena encircled with magnificent galleries, the members of schools from the different temples and wards throughout the city gathered. Over each was a presiding spirit whose movements were closely observed by those below them.

As I looked, I beheld innumerable groups of infants, whose shining robes presented every imaginable hue. In the hand of each was a rose. A small white dove rested upon each rose, and across its wings were written the words *Holiness to the LORD*.

Before each infant was an open scroll, upon which appeared to be written, in characters I could in no way understand, what had been their first lesson here. When all the infants were in their positions, they hovered calmly and motionless in the light near their guardian spirits. Each infant appeared to expect directions from the twelve spirits who were around the cross, upon whom they now fixed their attention. Oh, how blissful the silence that prevailed and that revealed the perfect order and divine harmony of the place!

Marietta's Unworthiness Revealed

"Listen, Marietta," said the angel, and with her right hand she pressed my temples. From that deep silence came forth music like the angelic breath of the most inward and holy life of the spirit. I could scarcely hear it as it moved over my inward being in softest melody. Until then, I had not known that within me were elements that could be awakened to such symphony or could vibrate to the touch of such sacred and interior melody. As the notes of that spirit of music arose, I thought a new nature was given me to enable me to realize harmony so perfect; I seemed to blend with it, until my own will sought to unite with it.

Then I felt the effects of my disordered soul. Note after note from the invisible source approached this inward life of mine but no longer moved in unison with the chords of my being. The music became harsh to me, in that I knew my dissimilarity to its nature. Then I suffered. Oh, the agony of that moment! The contrast was dreadful. Every part of my being was out of its proper state. The waves of harmony that moved softly and gently throughout the dome fell like disturbed waters onto my unworthy and contrary heart. I gladly would have escaped, for any other condition would have been preferable by far. I thought even the arena of mock worship would better agree with my nature, and there I could more easily harmonize with the prevailing law.

But I could not escape. I was a perfect wreck, and each moment made my condition more awful, until every hour seemed to be a year. At length I cried out, from the bitterness in my soul, "Oh, let me fly away from this scene! Other music has filled me with delight, other melodies have made me happy. I listened to it, and while I heard, I drank in the spirit of the sacred song. But now, by some unknown law, this harmonious sweetness reveals me in my unholy nature. All are witnesses of my discordance, and to myself I now appear unworthy for angelic association and lost beyond redemption. My spirit is wounded, broken, fallen; no part of it is adapted to another part of it. Oh, let me fly away to where darkness, with her black oppression, may hide me forever from myself.

"Oh, Angel! Veil this light that reveals my deformity, and save me from the torments of this angelic harmony. Is there a deeper hell? If demons were to gather around this lost spirit and mock it, they could do nothing to awaken new life in it; nothing else could crush this disjointed spiritual being with such a sense of its unworthiness."

Thus I pleaded to be released by some method from the light, the harmony, and the bliss that filled the great congregation to the utmost capacity of enjoyment. My suffering was beyond expression, and yet, at the time, I did not consider the cause to be anything more than the fact that my soul was disjointed. I realized my entire unworthiness for the employment, the society, and the happiness of the members of that paradise. On former occasions, I had desired to be admitted with them and to ever abide in that holy sanctuary, but I had not properly considered what qualifications I needed—which were presently lacking in me—in order to join them in their holy anthems. True, I had witnessed the deformity of the infant spirit and had with wonder beheld the operations of grace in its restoration, but never had I applied this knowledge to myself with understanding.

When I felt drawn by the sphere of darkness and saw the very cloud of death part to receive me, I looked up to the paradisical heaven with an earnest desire to enter there and be saved. But little did I know that even then, if I were permitted to enter as a member into the spirit thereof, I would suffer exceeding agony from the effects of the love and harmony of heaven upon me. My condition would involve me in perplexity and misery equal to the deepest hell. With this new knowledge, my mind quickly surveyed the entire scene, while pleading for relief. I was enabled to fully realize my condition and felt assured that all was lost and that I was doomed to misery.

At length an angel said, "Marietta, you are not lost. True, your deformity is exposed, and you are suffering because your spirit now discerns the true state of your discordant soul. By contrast to goodness, you are brought to a sense of what you lack. In this, perhaps, you will be better prepared to see the goodness of God in the provisions made for redemption through the Lord Jesus, whom all the heavens adore.

"When you were previously admitted into the society of the sanctified, your discordant condition was mostly hidden from your sight. You were, as a guest, permitted to receive the influence as an outer sacredness that, like holy dew, fell upon you and watered your thirsty spirit. But so perfect is the breath of holiness here that, when it touched your inner life, all your latent unworthiness appeared in contrast; hence your suffering. In this you are also, to a degree, enabled to discover the wisdom of a benevolent Creator in causing spirits of similar nature to dwell in similar places. The opposite elements of good and evil, therefore being separate, will not increase the misery or disturb the bliss of either.

"Thus it is revealed why no unclean thing can ever enter the Holy City that John the Revelator saw. Into this sacred temple no unholy, disembodied spirit can enter. Nor can any law of existence receive the impure, unsanctified soul within that city of spiritual life from which originated the soft, stirring melody that so much affected you. The inhabitants of this blessed abode could not dwell with spirits unreconciled to God in the spheres of darkness.

"Marietta, behold the goodness of God toward His creation. He would appear obviously unjust if He were to permit any law to operate that let even one of these little ones perish by being attracted into the deadly magnetism of the regions of misery and woe. Their tender and pure natures would writhe beneath the touch of the inflamed passions of those who are abandoned to the madness of insatiable desires. Indeed, God would be considered unjust if His law were to expose the innocent this way.

"In this the wisdom and goodness of God is displayed. No absolutely contrary element in the world of spirits mingles with the pure and harmonious. Thus, the sacred Scripture is fulfilled that says, when speaking of these conditions, *'He who is filthy, let him be filthy still; he who is righteous, let him be righteous still; he who is holy, let him be holy still'* (Rev. 22:11). In other words, let there be a separation between the qualities of good and evil with those who have departed from the flesh, let those who are holy enjoy that without the warring of evil elements, and let the unholy come together by their affinities. For it is justly written that an impassable gulf is fixed between good and evil (Luke 16:26), since these extremes can in no way blend.

"It is also written, *'Everyone who loves is born of God'* (1 John 4:7), and love has no likeness to hatred. Whoever is under the dominion of evil does not love God. If mortals only realized this law, they would strive against evil, cultivate righteousness in themselves, and thus through grace be prepared for the spiritual inheritance of the just. But, Marietta, you cannot now fully learn or comprehend this lesson. When these scenes are past, consider what you have witnessed and what the angels have taught you. Then learn and grow from these things, lest a greater evil should befall you than to realize an entire unworthiness for an everlasting inheritance with the Sanctified One.

"And when you are restored to the external world, look to Jesus, who alone can prepare you to return here and enjoy the rapture of heaven, and to join with the worshippers in this abode of the blessed. Here you have learned that the unregenerate cannot become the companions of these spirits. Do not weep, Marietta," said the angel, as I began to yield to grief. "Do not weep, for a Ransom is prepared. You may wash in a healing Fountain, by which all the impurity of your being may be removed. Rejoice greatly in this, since redemption is offered through great mercy, and because those who could not otherwise attain perfect joy are exalted from prison vaults to mansions in our Father's kingdom. For this grace, the saints in heaven praise God, and they do not cease day or night to utter hymns of thanksgiving to Him who is their Redeemer."

This being said, the angel touched my forehead. A stream of light entered my being, and I arose. "Now," said the angel, "you may listen to the soft notes of the song sung by the infants, who have just been admitted from the different temples of learning into this great center dome of the infant paradise of instruction."

The Song of Infants

The music of the infant choirs arose from their pure hearts with sweetness, filling the expanse and swelling into gentle waves, which harmoniously moved along the atmosphere above. Grandeur was added to the scene as I saw them formed into groups and uniting class with class—each class being composed of equal numbers, each spirit glowing with the holy fire of the sacred hymn.

Moving from group to group was a female spirit, clothed in garments pure and white. Upon her head was a crown set with gems, which shone with the brightness of the sun. In her left hand she held an open volume; in her right, a wand. She appeared to observe every infant and to clearly distinguish every voice, so as to know the relationship of their different qualities to each other. Likewise, her every movement was noticed by the infants, who sought to imitate her as earthly pupils try to imitate their teachers.

The parts of music performed were numerous yet in harmony, and the melody was the beauty of perfection. As they sang, their spirit fingers moved over their soft and mellow-toned harps, while all were increasingly inspired with confidence that, adding to the melody, appeared to blend them into one great soul, whose breath was the spirit and harmony of celestial love.

chapter 11

The Forlorn
and Doomed Being

❦

N ow another scene, varying in many parts,
was presented to the infants in the center
dome. They had congregated for the purpose
of preparing to advance to the superior plain, where
they were to begin a life of heavenly employment
and never ceasing rewards.

* * *

In order that you may better understand what I
relate and the purpose of the various representations before the infants, it is necessary to add that
one mode of instruction in the spirit world is to reveal principles through illustrations and scenes.

There is a law by which every principle, scene,
tragedy, person, creature, color, or substance in any
sphere that needs to be revealed can be cast back to
reflecting galleries as from a mirror. They can be
represented by panoramic and continuously revolving scenes, or they can be shown by persons performing the different parts like actors on a stage.

By these means, spirits uneducated in scientific
or artistic wisdom, in moral or spiritual laws, or in
the plan, structure, and movement of the intellectual, spiritual, moral, and physical universe, are

enabled to receive the intended impression so that they may discern the character of every idea, substance, thing, organism, or entity conveyed. So perfect are the representations that whatever is reflected becomes a part of the understanding.

To fully state the principles involved or to describe the varied scenes and illustrations employed, even in that primary school, is beyond my comprehension or capacity of narration. It would require volumes to contain their statements, were they written. I must therefore condense the story to a summary, and you must be content with the brief account I give.

* * *

As the new scene opened, the light and glory that illuminated the dome gradually withdrew, until a twilight—like that which follows the setting sun on an autumn evening—set the outlines of the city in bold relief against the sky. All was silent, every being was motionless, and nothing relieved the stillness of the moment except the sweet whispering of a soft and gentle breeze that glided over and through the vast plain.

After this great change in the appearance of everything around, and a brief pause, there appeared a portion of earth resembling a moonlit landscape. In this was represented a subterraneous abyss where a human lay wounded in many places and was apparently dying. He lay beneath overhanging clouds, which were burdened with gloom. Upon this person who was struggling as if seeking relief from his suffering, every spirit fixed its ardent attention.

His efforts were fitful and convulsive but in no way adapted to his needs, and his inability to remove himself was clearly manifested in his demeanor. He strove to heal his wounds by administering what he thought to be antidotes but that proved to be inadequate when tested. If possible, those supposed remedies only enhanced his suffering and added to his peril. He used various instruments by which he hoped to discern the pathway leading from his gloomy abode, and he attempted to build a passage across the abyss that encircled him. But all failed, and he fell back in utter despair. Then he sought to be reconciled to his fate.

While he lay languishing and helpless, I saw a group gather around him. There was an elderly female, along with youths and children. They appeared to grieve on his account and endeavored to give him some relief. They tried to bind up his wounds, to raise his drooping head, and to restore vitality throughout, but all to no effect. He still groaned and weakened. I now saw that he lay more directly upon the brink of the abyss and that he drew nearer to it each moment, as if moved by an invisible and irresistible power.

Oh, the intensity of that moment! The elderly female drew near and, clasping her arms around his neck, sought to remove him from his fearful condition. The youths united with her in the effort, but all in vain. Still he drew nearer to the abyss. I also saw that his body manifested the increasing effects of his malady, until every part was one diseased mass. Finally yielding to the destroyer, he lay senseless.

Then, to my surprise, the man's spirit arose from his physical body. As it stood above the prostrate form, the spirit was even more deformed and dreadful. Spiritual and moral disease was worked throughout and controlled each part with unyielding power.

The body and spirit were not separated; they still depended on each other. Where the body had failed to express grief, the spirit, as a separate entity, was capable of fully displaying it. And so the spirit gave full expression of the suffering of the being. As the body had yielded to the power of disease and pain, so the spirit also finally weakened under the malady that was working within and throughout.

While thus suffering, the spirit looked up, as if to petition aid from above, but a cloud of thick darkness overshadowed it. Then it looked wildly around, evidently seeking some place of refuge or source of relief. When this resulted as before, the spirit sank away, as if yielding in absolute despair to the power of unending wretchedness. As hope declined, the eyes of the spirit vacantly fell, and in looking downward, he discovered an abyss yawning below. Then the spirit again convulsed and sought to escape, but in vain.

The scene was horrible. The agonizing, fruitless efforts and the manifestation of final despair combined to present a scene of wretchedness beyond human description. Suddenly the spirit disappeared, and the man's body gave signs of returning life and perception. But he only recovered to know again his excessive misery in the outer man and to more fully feel his forlorn state.

The group standing around him, encouraged by the manifestation of returning life, renewed their efforts to restore him. This, too, was futile. They had no power to alleviate his grief or to restore the lost health of body or spirit. While they thus struggled, a light descended, and I saw that they were in the same condition of body and spirit, except that the effect had not yet manifested itself in them so completely. Nevertheless, the result was equally as certain. They began to perceive this, at which point they exclaimed, "Is there no help?"

"No help in the arm of flesh" (see 2 Chronicles 32:8), answered a voice familiar to me, but I did not know from where it came. *"Can the Ethiopian change his skin or the leopard its spots?"* (Jer. 13:23), continued that voice. "How will the unstrung instrument tune itself? Indeed, how will the dying, those who are already victims, restore departing vitality? Will they escape the doom awaiting them by the strength of their exhausted energies? No, wherever they go, there is no relief. Help must descend from above, or hope will not appear."

The Vision Explained

As the scene closed, an angel addressed the multitude, saying, "The gloomy region just revealed is a view of earth, the birthplace of mortals. Observe the forlorn being of man, who suffers innumerable ills—physical, moral, and spiritual—and who often struggles to overcome and to rise above them. His ineffective efforts reveal his inability to save himself.

"The spirit that arose when the body yielded represents the immortal nature that, though the body perish, will exist in a more acutely sensitive state. Its sinking in despair portrays the great truth

101

that the death of the body can in no way relieve the soul from moral or spiritual degradation.

"The group of friends represents human sympathy, which inclines members of the race to seek relief from sorrow by mutual aid. Sympathy is the principle that prompts the more benevolent and philanthropic to devise means and to pursue plans for the alleviation of the sufferings of man.

"Those who indulge this principle feel another's woe. They deeply sympathize with those who endure pain and anguish from whatever cause. But being in a similar condition, they fail to remove evil from the world and to elevate man through human schemes and in their own strength, though apparent relief may inspire transient hope. For this reason, earth's reformers have encountered repeated failures until, disheartened, they sink into despair and are often finally led to discover some fundamental lack in themselves.

"It has been this way with man from age to age. Centuries have succeeded centuries, and each has had its philanthropists who have struggled through a weary existence without attaining their goal.

"Often the race, to human appearances, has approached the dawn of a better day, and those who have labored for such have sung earth's jubilee. But before they have emerged from the gloomy plains, they have felt the triumph of innate disease. The ground upon which they stood has yielded to the pressure, and the muscles upon which they relied have relaxed and have lost their strength. The rock has become sliding sands, and the strength of their hope and effort has become weakness. Thus, when they have supposed victory has been won and the heights have been attained, sudden quaking has seized their minds and thrown them into a still deeper abyss.

"It will always be so, until men cleave to the Lord, who alone is a sure defense and *"a stronghold in the day of trouble"* (Nah. 1:7); upon whose shoulders rests the government of all things (Isa. 9:6); and in whom, and by whom, all things have their being (Rom. 11:36). The voice that, from above, declared that help was not in the arm of flesh was the voice of Truth, which ever seeks to reveal to man his true condition, to awaken him to a sense of his degradation, and to urge the doctrine of salvation through the Lord Jesus."

Then raising his eyes toward the superior heavens, the angel, in a meek, fervent, and exalted manner, said, "Father of all, let Your Spirit inspire these infant minds with understanding, so that they may behold with profit the scenes that reveal the effects of sin in the world of discord from which they have come. Also inspire them with the wonders of Your love in the means of salvation.

"Endow them with supporting grace while they behold the trials that accompany their Redeemer's mission and His passion while He suffers the cruelty of those He seeks to save. Grant, O Lord our Redeemer, that these may be prepared to arise through degrees of life and understanding to the heaven of youths, where Your glory is revealed in greater degrees of paradisical light, love, and ecstatic beatitudes.

"Let Your will be done by angels who delight to lead upward the little ones whom You have entrusted to their charge, so that Your glory may be reflected upon them in a manner well pleasing in Your sight. Then their spiritual understanding will be enlarged; the love principles of their beings will be unfolded; and Your name, O Savior of men, You who are all and in all to us, the ministering servants of Your grace, will be glorified in them evermore."

"Evermore, amen," responded the guardian angels and instructors. "Evermore, evermore, amen," the heavenly atmosphere re-accented until the echo expired in the distance.

chapter 12

The Babe of Bethlehem

After a brief pause, a voice said, as if from a distance, "Be instructed by what is given. Truths connected with your race are revealed to your understanding. Receive the principles. Seek to comprehend."

Then the choristers, touching their golden lyres, chanted with loud voices, "*'Glory to God in the highest, and on earth peace, goodwill toward men!'* (Luke 2:14). *'Behold,* [we] *bring you good tidings of great joy which will be to all people. For there is born to you this day in the city of David a Savior, who is Christ the Lord'* (vv. 10–11)."

Then, beneath a pale light, Bethlehem, the birthplace of the Redeemer, was revealed. The condition of the infants in paradise—moving in the very glory of divine life, blessed by the Redeemer, sanctified with His love, greeted by choirs of the heavenly spheres, and attended by angels expressly appointed —reflected a state greatly in contrast to that now being revealed, in which was represented the dreary world and the circumstances attending the memorable event of the birth of Jesus of Nazareth.

While Mary, the mother of Jesus, held in her arms the infant through whom alone salvation could appear to men and in whom was revealed the untold goodness and love of God, her humble condition reflected the truth so clearly that not only the infants but also all the angels beholding the scene manifested great emotion. After a short pause, the angel who had before urged the truths revealed, said, "Behold the birthplace of the Redeemer, even Jesus whose glory illuminates this temple. For you the Spirit of redemption assumed this humble form. Through the Savior's humiliation, heavenly mansions are prepared for all who trust in His grace and are obedient to the law of redemption. Adore Him, for He is worthy."

"We will adore Him evermore," said the chief guardian, and the infants repeated, "We will adore Him." Then all was silent once again. The scene more plainly revealed Mary, meekly resting on Joseph, who pressed her to his heart while she gently held the babe of Bethlehem. Near them were a few Israelites in humble attitude, steadily looking upon the babe and His mother. Around them was an innumerable company of angels, invisible to mortal vision. These held their crowns in their hands, while their harps, which were untouched and silent, lay before them. Above them rested a cloud of glory, and out of that cloud proceeded a voice saying, *"This is My beloved Son"* (Matt. 3:17).

Another voice said, "This day the love of God is manifested to man, who is fallen, who is *"dead in trespasses and sins"* (Eph. 2:1). Now salvation appears. Now truth moves from the eternity of its existence, clothed in the garments of salvation (Isa. 61:10). Justice and Mercy meet upon the fallen planet, and they embrace over prostrate humanity. Justice declares itself against sin. Thus the eternal throne is vindicated, and the government of the kingdom is perpetuated. Meanwhile, Mercy pleads the cause of the sinner, who is exposed to unremitting sorrow because of transgression."

"Let us bow down and adore the God of our salvation," said the chief guardian, and all assumed a humble attitude. Another voice from above spoke, saying, "It is fitting that you worship, that you bow down while infinite condescension is being revealed. Let all heaven adore Him in this manner." The humble attitude of the angels and the infant spirits added greatly to the solemnity of the occasion. Surely there was reverence—sincere acknowledgement of mercies bestowed.

I was reflecting upon the true devotion manifested by the worshippers, when the chief guardian said, "We will arise. Behold, a new scene draws near." Raising her eyes toward the higher heaven, she continued, "Be our help, O our Father, in whose life we exist, so that we may understand what heaven reveals for our instruction, and so that we may know Your love and be prepared to do Your will evermore."

"Amen," responded every infant, led by their separate guardians.

Justice and Mercy

The former objects had passed away during the worship of the angels and the infants, and new ones appeared. A bright cloud rested a little above the temple, and from that cloud descended a being who appeared omnipotent in strength. The name *Justice* was written upon his majestic brow. His movement was like that of a ruler at whose bidding worlds might flee away and in whose hand universal law might pause and slumber.

This august personage advanced toward a gloomy glen, encircled by huge mountains whose lofty peaks ascended far into the blue vault above. His demeanor indicated purpose.

As he drew very near what appeared to be the object of his pursuit, a dark cloud moved down the mountains, attended by lightning in all the terror of wild display, as if electric fountains were issuing from an ocean of volcanic elements. Heavy thunderings shook the base of the massive hills. Fire, smoke, and tempest were emitted, while the elements seemed to madly embrace each other. The scene was frightfully terrific; even so, Justice advanced, and the lightning bolts seemed to entwine themselves into a diadem around his brow.

The name *Destruction* was now mirrored in super-flaming letters in the lightning upon the clouds. This name was repeated by the stunning peals of thunder. Beneath this awful display of angry elements and the movement of Justice, the earth began to quake and give way.

At this moment, when the excitement had apparently reached its climax, a voice of lamentation came from beneath the cloud and at the foot of the mountain—a voice of despair, saying, "Spare us! Is there no hope?"

"No hope," echoed the thunders, and Justice still advanced. "No hope," he repeated, as he raised his hand of might.

"No hope, no hope," chimed the hoarse voice of contending elements. "We perish without hope," said the voice of wailing that grew weaker and more suppressed. "Alas! We perish unpitied!" In an instant was revealed the forlorn being and the afflicted group displayed in a former scene.

The trembling female bent over the prostrate man, as if to screen him from the tempest. But as she saw Justice raise his mighty hand, she fell back, exclaiming, "All is lost! No hope! We perish! Receive us, you abyss!"

The suspense of that moment was dreadful. Justice still advanced, as if to cut in pieces and to crush the forlorn man whose trembling hands were raised in supplication. By his side and around him his group of friends, who had fallen, were as helpless and imploring as he was.

At this moment, a voice from the burning cloud said, "The moral law has been violated and has therefore been disordered in you, O man. Did you think you could trifle with it and not suffer the consequences? Do you not understand that the law, when opposed, brings about the destruction of the body in which it is violated? Moral law is the law of wisdom and goodness. Have you not violated it? Indeed, you have. Now the dreadful effects ensue, and you are the sufferer."

As this voice ceased, a great light flashed over the scene, and an exceedingly bright cloud descended from above. From this cloud and with the speed of thought, there came another being, the very image of meekness, whose demeanor was the opposite of Justice.

Embracing Justice, who was still advancing toward the fallen group, this second being said, "Are you relentless, you who vindicates the everlasting throne? Must the sinner perish? Is there no hope?"

"No hope in the arm of flesh," answered Justice in a voice that shook the firmament above. The stars trembled, and the earth quaked and reeled as the words proceeded from his lips. "No hope or cause of hope exists on the fallen planet," repeated Justice, still advancing. As the blow was about to descend upon the sinner, the being who hung upon the neck of Justice bent over that bleeding form. Placing her left hand on his heart, this being raised her right hand, and touching the arm of Justice, said, *"'Your throne, O God, is forever and ever'* (Ps. 45:6). Your kingdom is from everlasting to everlasting (Ps. 145:13). Your Word endures (1 Pet. 1:25). To Your years there is no end (Ps. 102:27). You, O God, are holy (Ps. 22:3). Righteousness is the foundation of Your throne (Ps. 97:2), the pavilion of Your dwelling place, the glory of the everlasting hills, the defense and safety of the heaven of heavens, where congregate the innumerable myriads of glorified seraphim.

"Here, O God, is a fallen being. Sin is the violation of Your law. This sinner has presumed upon Your government and has touched the flaming sword (see Genesis 3:24) with impious hands; he has dared vengeance, trifled with Your will, and contended with eternal and irrevocable justice. He has fallen. He lies bruised, mangled, and dying. Yet, O God, You have created him an immortal being. He is intellectual and therefore accountable. He is spiritual, and because of sin he lies on the verge of a bottomless abyss, where, if he falls, he will feel immortal pangs and dwell in unremitting woe. The reed is bruised, but not entirely broken; the flickering blaze of the smoking flax, though expiring, still exists. (See Isaiah 42:3.) Mercy is my name.

Mercy is an attribute of Your throne. To You, O God, belong Justice and Mercy. Let Your love descend, O Eternal One! And you, Justice, spare this fallen being! Spare him, though he has sinned and has traded his eternal good for a morsel!" (See Hebrews 12:16-17.)

Here Mercy bowed her head, as if to await the decision. A voice from the cloud said, "Mercy, you have pleaded for the sinner, and heaven gives audience. Can you find a ransom? Justice, pause in your execution of punishment."

Then another voice said, "*'God so loved the world that He gave His only begotten Son'* (John 3:16). By My righteous servant I will justify many. He will bear their iniquities." (See Isaiah 53:11.)

Then there was a pause, during which a female approached from the right. It was Mary, whom I had seen holding the babe of Bethlehem. She bowed by the expiring form and, by the aid of Mercy, extended the babe over it. She then looked up toward the cloud with reverence, and the voice continued, "*'This is My beloved Son, in whom I am well pleased'* (Matt. 3:17). *'A bruised reed He will not break, and smoking flax He will not quench, till He sends forth justice to victory; and in His name Gentiles will trust'* (Matt. 12:20-21)."

Then Justice replied, "Has this little child endured temptation and *'suffered outside the gate'* (Heb. 13:12)? Has He conquered death? Can He hold back the tempest of warring elements? Can He change the malignant nature of that perverted heart? Can He descend the maelstrom of death and stop the heavy tide whose broad current rolls to the bottomless abyss?"

Then Mercy said, "The future will answer you, you who hold the balances of equity, the scales of universal right."

When Mercy had answered, the scene changed, and upon the mount, called the Mount of Olives, I saw a Being lovelier than the sons of men. He lifted up His eyes to heaven and said, *"Behold, I have come; in the volume of the book it is written of Me; to do Your will, O God"* (Heb. 10:7).

Then appeared a vast multitude of deformed beings exhibiting every type of human suffering and shameful depravity. Addressing them, He said, *"'If anyone thirsts, let him come to Me and drink'* (John 7:37). *'I am the way, the truth, and the life. No one comes to the Father except through Me'* (John 14:6)." At this point another voice said, "This is *'the Hope of Israel'* (Jer. 14:8), *'the Offspring of David, the Bright and Morning Star'* (Rev. 22:16). Now arises *'the Sun of Righteousness'* (Mal. 4:2). Now appears Truth in its redeeming glory from the Eternal Cause. Look unto Him, you who perish, for He comes to redeem."

Again I saw the mangled form. These words had fallen upon his dull and heavy hearing, and although he scarcely understood them, he raised his eyes as if to see from where hope had been offered. And as he looked, He who stood upon the Mount descended and bowed over him saying, "What do you desire?" The sufferer replied, "That I might find salvation." Then answered the Person bending over him, "I came to seek and save the lost." (See Luke 19:10.) Then said Justice to Mercy, "Is this your ransom?" And another voice said, *"Behold! The Lamb of God who takes away the sin of the world!"* (John 1:29). And He who offered redemption said, *"For this cause I have come into the world"* (John 18:37). Then an angel said, "By Your stripes the sinner is healed." (See Isaiah 53:5; 1 Peter 2:24.)

Justice spoke, saying, "Has He prevailed?" Then he said to Mercy, "You plead the sinner's cause. But until He whom you propose as Redeemer approaches the fallen, holding in His hand these contending elements, He will not rescue anyone. Do you still seek the fallen being's salvation, his restoration to harmony?"

"Yes," answered Mercy, "for this I intercede."

chapter 13

The Betrayal

❧

Another scene appeared, and I realized again how inefficient are all means of communication to reveal its true character to human minds. First I saw that same lovely Being seated around a table with a group of His friends. One of them leaned upon Him and, in pure love's tenderest expression, looked up into His face while listening to the words that fell from His lips. Filled with exceeding sorrow, the group looked upon Him as He said, *"Assuredly, I say to you, one of you will betray Me"* (Matt. 26:21). After this He took bread, blessed it, and broke it. Giving it to them He said, *"Take, eat; this is My body which is broken for you"* (1 Cor. 11:24). He then took the cup, gave thanks, and gave it to them, saying,

> *Drink from it, all of you. For this is My blood of the new covenant, which is shed for many for the remission of sins. But I say to you, I will not drink of this fruit of the vine from now on until that day when I drink it new with you in My Father's kingdom.* (Matt. 26:27–29)

Then I heard a mighty angel, whose voice was like the utterance of Nature when her forces contend, saying,

The Betrayal

The Son of Man indeed goes just as it is written of Him, but woe to that man by whom the Son of Man is betrayed! It would have been good for that man if he had not been born.   *(Matt. 26:24)*

Many millions then broke forth in unison, saying, "Woe to that man, it would have been good for him not to have been born. Woe, woe, woe to that man!" The elements of the interior shook like the leaves of a forest when contending with autumnal tempests. As the echoes of these awful utterances ceased, the small group at the table arose. After they had sung a solemn hymn, they withdrew.

Then I saw one of them step away from the group, silently and unperceived, as they retired slowly and solemnly from the scene of the Last Supper. As this one advanced, his movement changed; his step was quick and excited, his face showed an inward commotion that burned with consuming fires—fires kindled in the soul by antagonistic elements.

I wondered at this. I could not perceive by what means a transition so sudden and so great could be brought about. Just before, I had seen him seated with his friends, and those friends were suffering greatly because of the predictions of Him to whom they looked for counsel and for safety. They mourned, fearing His departure from them. They leaned on Him as a dependent child leans on a faithful parent. They had hoped—indeed, they had raised high their hope in Him. The extent or exact nature of that hope I could not comprehend. Still I saw that they greatly depended on Him for future good or great achievements. When His words indicating His

115

departure had been spoken, the men had fallen into despair, and perfect wretchedness possessed them when He declared that one of them would betray Him. I heard them in the deepest apprehension inquire, "Lord, is it I? Lord, is it I?" That had been an awful moment, a moment that tried the soul, a moment in which gloom gathered around them as a blanket of thick darkness.

In their spirits they grieved when He said the following:

> *A little while, and you will not see Me; and again a little while, and you will see Me, because I go to the Father.*   *(John 16:16)*

> *But because I have said these things to you, sorrow has filled your heart. Nevertheless I tell you the truth. It is to your advantage that I go away; for if I do not go away, the Helper will not come to you; but if I depart, I will send Him to you.*
>   *(vv. 6–7)*

> *I will not leave you comfortless: I will come to you.*   *(John 14:18 KJV)*

> *Let not your heart be troubled; you believe in God, believe also in Me. In My Father's house are many mansions; if it were not so, I would have told you. I go to prepare a place for you. And if I go and prepare a place for you, I will come again and receive you to Myself; that where I am, there you may be also....A little while longer and the world will see Me no more, but you will see Me. Because I live, you will live also.*   *(vv. 1–3, 19)*

> *Most assuredly, I say to you that you will weep and lament, but the world will rejoice; and you*

will be sorrowful, but your sorrow will be turned into joy....Therefore you now have sorrow; but I will see you again and your heart will rejoice, and your joy no one will take from you....These things I have spoken to you in figurative language; but the time is coming when I will no longer speak to you in figurative language, but I will tell you plainly about the Father.

(John 16:20, 22, 25)

They believed these words of promise and consolation that He spoke while predicting His departure. Still, they were sad and exceedingly sorrowful because He said, "I am going away." They loved Him; He was worthy of all holy affection.

His words were full of goodness. There was so much heavenly love, tenderness, and paternal care manifested by Him that I wondered what reason could be sufficient to cause any one of them to betray into the hands of enemies a Being whose presence thus inspired hope, love, reverence, and adoration.

While my spirit pondered this, I heard the angels who instructed the infants say, "In what you see, behold the nature of good and evil contrasted. That little group was the company of the Lord's disciples who partook of the Passover with Him on the evening before His betrayal. He who addressed them was the Redeemer who, knowing that His 'hour' was at hand and also who would betray Him, prepared their minds for the trial and predicted the events that were to follow. He who so strangely withdrew was Judas Iscariot, who betrayed his Master for thirty pieces of silver. (See Matthew 26:14–16.)

"If you observe this scene more carefully as it passes, you will see the two great principles that are operative with man in a fallen state. They will so unfold themselves to you that the solemn truths revealed will be grafted into your being."

Judas before the Council

The angel withdrew, and Judas appeared and was seen entering a council chamber. There were gathered the chief priests and elders of ancient Israel who, at the time of the Lord's passion, conspired to take Him, put Him to death, and thus bring perpetual scorn and disgrace upon Him. The spirit of Judas was the opposite of that which had appeared in the room set apart for the Last Supper. How entirely changed! His outward expression now spoke of inward rage—the rage of a malicious heart, a heart grievously treacherous and desperately wicked. (See Jeremiah 17:9.)

At this time a pale light flashed over his head, revealing a group of demon spirits. These urged him onward by their vindictive inspiration. They manifested all that can be imagined of the evil that composes the Arch-deceiver, the foe of all good, the destroyer of peace, the instigator of crime, the enemy of right, the soul-alluring Satan. These demons poured forth their hellish magnetism, and by the power of their wills they overwhelmed him with the hate they desired to manifest toward the Son of Man.

As Judas entered the mock sanctuary, the priests arose and greeted him with smiles—smiles inspired by malice that had a hope of revenge. Then the chief priests, addressing him, said, "Welcome Judas, friend of right, friend of God's ancient church, the law of Moses, and the people of this ecclesiastic kingdom. He whom the masses call Jesus, and whom His followers call the King of the Jews by His own declaration, has long been worthy of death. He has sought the destruction of this beloved city, the city especially favored by God. He has prophesied to destroy the great temple, to put down the authority of the church, to change laws and customs, and to establish His own kingdom upon the ruin of Jehovah's kingdom.

"This man calls Himself God. He is a blasphemer against high heaven, and He mocks the throne of the Eternal One. He presumes to call us hypocrites. Even those whom God has, by His right hand, exalted as teachers in Israel, He calls *"blind leaders of the blind"* (Matt. 15:14). Though we have the keys of the kingdom, He has accused us of keeping those who are willing from entering. He has charged us with a love of sin, a love of power, and a vile nature. Surely He is worthy of death."

"Indeed, worthy of the most ignominious death," came the corresponding verdict from all who were present.

"This Man is drawing with Him the credulous, the ignorant, the dreamers, and those who are dissatisfied with the church," continued one of the priests. "By His peculiar nature, adapted to work wonders, He has deceived many who are worthy of a better calling." Then, addressing his friends, he continued: "But these people will soon become conscious of His false character. It will be well for him who first reveals to us the true character of this vile deceiver and who enables us to bring Him before the people. Upon this person, the nation will bestow great honors, and lasting blessings will be upon his head."

"And lasting blessings will be upon his head," repeated the associate priests.

This was sufficient to inspire Judas with the desire of being first in the undertaking. So he proposed, in the presence of them all, to deliver his Master into the hands of anyone the priest would then commission for that purpose. He would do so upon the condition that had been previously considered: his receiving thirty pieces of silver.

Jesus Prays in the Garden

Again the scene changed. The cover of evening overshadowed that portion of earth. A little way from the busy multitude, He who had counseled His disciples was moving slowly along with three of His chosen. He was sorrowful. I can never forget that scene. Oh, the loveliness that was manifested! Truly I thought Him *"chief among ten thousand"* (Song 5:10), and the One *"altogether lovely"* (v. 16). Still He suffered. They paused, and He said, *"My soul is exceedingly sorrowful, even to death. Stay here and watch with Me....Watch and pray, lest you enter into temptation"* (Matt. 26:38, 41). He then left them, went a little farther, and fell to the ground. While bowing on the cold earth, enduring the deepest agony, He prayed more earnestly and *"His sweat became like great drops of blood falling down to the ground"* (Luke 22:44).

Above Him the heavens opened, and legions of angels appeared, apparently clothed in garments of mourning. They veiled their faces as they bent over the Garden of Gethsemane, in which their Lord suffered. All was silent, mournfully silent. Each angel beheld the scene with wonder. There was Christ the Lord, the divine Man, He whose name is written in the Scriptures as *"Wonderful, Counselor, Mighty God, Everlasting Father, Prince of Peace"* (Isa. 9:6).

While I observed the Savior in His agony, a cloud descended, resting over the Redeemer. In the cloud were Justice and Mercy. With intense interest they observed the scene below.

At length the Savior prayed, saying: *"O My Father, if it is possible, let this cup pass from Me; nevertheless, not as I will, but as You will"* (Matt. 26:39). Then Mercy said to Justice, "Here is the Ransom."

Again He prayed, *"O My Father, if this cup cannot pass away from Me unless I drink it, Your will be done"* (v. 42). Then there descended a mighty angel, who stood by Him and strengthened Him.

Then Mercy said to Justice, "Behold the Offering."

Jesus Taken as a Prisoner

The hour of suffering having passed, Jesus arose. When He reached His disciples and found them asleep, He said to them, *"Are you still sleeping and resting? It is enough! The hour has come; behold, the Son of Man is being betrayed into the hands of sinners"* (Mark 14:41).

My guide said to me, "Behold, in Jesus, an example of meek submission. From His sympathy with the disordered and dying race, He agonized beneath the burden of human woe. Though just, He suffered because of an adopted affinity with the unjust, and still you heard Him say, *'Not as I will, but as You will'* (Matt. 26:39); *'Not My will, but Yours* [O God], *be done'* (Luke 22:42).

"This was needed, so that man might have grace bestowed, so that he might become united to heavenly spheres by the power of love, and so that he might thus be exalted from degradation to mansions of righteousness and peace, prepared in heaven for the ransomed of the Lord. But, Marietta, you will soon behold the contrast; in what is to pass before you, the true condition of the perverted heart will be unfolded."

Again my attention was directed to a dark and melancholy scene. Below me I saw a heavy cloud, which was agitated as if burdened with the spirit of disputing elements. Discordant sounds arose from the midst thereof. They were hard to understand, and at first the cause was hidden from me. But at length I heard, as if from the voice of an excited mob, the enthusiastic inquiry, "Where will we find Him? Hurry, most worthy guide, to the place of His retreat. Time wastes away, and the leaders of the people demand that the 'outlaw' be found. He *will* perish."

"Indeed, He will perish, and very soon," clamored a multitude who were, while moving toward Jesus and His disciples, enveloped in a cloud that overhung their pathway. The contrast between the scenes was so great that I was terrified. Turning to my guide, I inquired, "Who are these who disturb the stillness of this solemn hour? Can you inform me where they come from and where they are going? Of whom do they speak in language so excited, and with a determination so destructive?"

"These," she said, "are a band of soldiers from the chief priests and elders of the Jews. The object of their revengeful pursuit is Jesus, who, in the agony of His soul, prayed in the garden."

"What has He done to excite such envy?" I exclaimed.

"He has preached the year of the Lord and announced the mission of God's only Son to the world. (See Luke 4:18–21.) He has given sight to the blind, restored hearing to the deaf, healed the sick, raised the dead, comforted the mourner, instructed the ignorant, and pleaded with the despisers of the mercy of God to regard the Creator of heaven and earth as their Sovereign, their rightful Lawgiver, and their Redeemer."

"And is this why they seek to destroy Him?" I inquired. "Has He ever contended with them?"

"Have you not read in the sacred Scriptures what the prophet said, when moved by the Holy Spirit, concerning One who would come: *'Behold! My Servant whom I have chosen, My Beloved in whom My soul is well pleased! I will put My Spirit upon Him, and He will declare justice to the Gentiles. He will not quarrel nor cry out, nor will anyone hear His voice in the streets'* (Matt. 12:18–19)? This Jesus— God manifest in the flesh—who bowed in humble prayer and whom the people seek to destroy as a vile outlaw, is He of whom the prophet spoke."

While the angel continued to speak, the exasperated multitude, armed with swords and clubs, approached Jesus and His disciples. They were led by Judas Iscariot, who had sat with Him at the Last

Supper and who had proposed to deliver Jesus to the chief priests and elders of the people. As they drew near, I saw above Judas a mighty angel of darkness, from whom issued a pale, hellish flame that encompassed him and burned in his nerves like living fire. With wild determination, Judas advanced and hailed Jesus as his friend and Lord, sealing his mockery and heartless treachery with a kiss.

But Jesus appeared to fully understand his intentions and said to him, *"Friend, why have you come?"* (Matt. 26:50). And to the multitude He said, *"'Have you come out, as against a robber, with swords and clubs to take Me? I sat daily with you, teaching in the temple, and you did not seize Me'* (v. 55). *'Therefore, if you seek Me, let these* [who believe in Me] *go their way'* (John 18:8). *'For this cause I have come into the world'* (v. 37)."

Then one of the multitude answered, "Tell us for what cause."

Jesus replied, "That salvation might be given to the world, and that all, even those who attack Me, might, through faith and repentance, enter into rest. Into your hands I submit Myself, but no harm will befall these My disciples."

Then said the mockers, "You are our prisoner; we bear You before the tribunals of the people, and no one helps You. How can You say of these Your disciples, 'No harm shall befall them'?" And with cruel hands, they led Him away.

At this the disciples fled, each one his own way, and forsook Him, except for one who followed his Lord even to the hall of judgment.

chapter 14

Cruelties Inflicted upon Jesus

As Jesus was led away amid the shouts of the multitude, I turned and looked upon the infants and angelic spectators, who appeared to be more afflicted than at any former period. I then inquired, "Can there be sorrow in heaven? Do angels weep?"

I heard a voice say, "Marietta, your question is a valid one. Angels have hearts to feel. Who in heaven could witness the betrayal of the Savior of sinners without pouring out his soul in sad expressions?"

"Amen!" uttered ten thousand voices.

The voice continued, saying, "And who can endure the sight? Behold the innocent Sufferer. See! They beat Him as they hurry Him along the rugged way. They mock, they deride Him; they treat Him cruelly. Let all the heavens pause as they behold the mournful scene, for the Redeemer suffers in the hands of sinners. Awake, you spirit sympathies! Behold, Divine Good whom angels adore is *'despised and rejected by men'* (Isa. 53:3)."

As the voice ceased, I heard another angel say, "Behold! Angels descend from the highest heavens!"

I then beheld, far above the vast assembly that witnessed the scene, an innumerable company of superior beings. They had palm branches in their hands and crowns upon their heads. Their crowns represented the starry heavens, being miniature expressions of the wreathed universes that encircle the throne of the Infinite One. As these beings drew near, a dazzling light preceded them. This light pervaded the spiritual atmosphere and was so exalted in its nature that the angels who had composed the former audience could not continually behold it. The approach of this light so revealed the imperfection of my nature that I sought to conceal myself, but nothing could be concealed in that holy light.

I gladly would have fled, but I had no power to carry out that desire. "Surely," I said in my mind, "if this is only a manifestation of what is in the higher heavens, how can mortals ever reach that divine abode? How can vile man hope to enter the glory that, to the unprepared soul, would surely become a consuming fire?"

While thus reflecting, I heard one of the cherubic beings say, "Angels, kindred spirits, inhabitants of the exalted heavens, bow down before your Lord, for He is worthy. Adore Him from the deep and immortal sentiment of your revering spirits, for all angels delight to offer praises to Him. He is worthy of all adoration. Praise Him! Praise the Lord, the Redeemer of earth! While fallen beings mockingly gather around Him and impiously hail Him as King, let the harmonious universe be moved with reverence, and let all spiritual beings adore Him."

Then each bowed down in silent adoration of the Lord, while feeble and bewildered men hurried Him to the judgment hall. As the angels declared Him God manifested in the flesh, I wondered still the more why, having so much power, He did not exert it and subdue those who sought to destroy Him. Also, there were myriads of mighty angels, each having apparent capacity to disperse at will those who led their Lord away, and I wondered why they did not seek to avert the impending storm.

Perceiving my thoughts, the instructor said, "He came to seek and save (Luke 19:10), not to destroy (Matt. 5:17). He endures the scoffs of the wicked, and offers Himself as a ransom for sinners (1 Tim. 2:5–6). By His submission, He fulfills the prophecy that says, '*A bruised reed He will not break* [meaning, He will not harm the helpless], *and smoking flax He will not quench* [meaning, He will not extinguish the life or hope of man]' (Matt. 12:20). His is a mission of redemption, not of judgment and execution."

Then I heard voices as the going forth of many waters, saying, "Be amazed, O Earth, for your sins have brought upon you unspeakable woe. Pity has prompted the offering, and your Redeemer groans beneath the load."

Then Mercy said to Justice, "As it is written, '*God so loved the world that He gave His only begotten Son*' (John 3:16). This is the Ransom. In Jesus the nations of earth will have hope. Behold the Offering! In this Offering there is a principle for the removal of sin and unholiness, a principle intended to establish sympathy between the depraved race and the life that is above."

Then said the angel to the infants, "This is your Redeemer. In Him alone is the Life that can quicken and save, and by Him you were admitted into this paradise. Let each observe the scene as it advances, for by it heaven intends to give an impression that will enable all to estimate, according to their capacity, the value of the Redeemer to them." While the angel addressed them, their expressions of sympathy displayed the purity of their beings and the tenderness and emotion with which they had observed the suffering Son.

Then all with one accord said, "How will we utter praises and thanksgivings to God for this gift, the gift of life through His only begotten Son, our Savior? Can we not relieve Him? Can we not share His woe? He is in the midst of His foes. They do not know Him. They give Him unwarranted pain. Who can endure the sight? Let us fly to His relief! He is our Redeemer!" Such exclamations fell from the holy lips of the occupants of the infant paradise.

One of the mighty angels then said, "He is our Lord; He makes the heavens harmonious with the perfection of His being, and melodious with the music of His speech. He makes bliss to arise as the golden morning and to shed its holy luster and divine goodness upon the workmanship of His hands. Indeed, the heavens declare His precious name, and the peopled expanse vibrates with the soft and gentle cadence of His outflowing love. Yet, in the form of divine Man, we behold Him hurried onward by fallen beings as they bear Him toward the haughty Sanhedrin of a heartless church—a church where Jehovah is named in empty words but is not worshipped." Like the voice of one man, the innumerable multitude uttered, "Let us arise and beat back the mockers of the Lord!"

"No," said another voice. It was Justice, standing in a cloud of exceeding brightness. In his right hand he held the seven thunders, from which sprang lightnings and tempest, and these spanned the globe and enveloped the race—both small and great, the living and the dead—in their awful cloud. It shook the foundation of earth and caused the souls of men to quake with the greatness of the terror of the rolling thunder and blackening tempests.

Lying before the angel was the deformed being that was revealed to me earlier, wounded nearly unto death, and the blood from his wounds stained the earth on which he lay. Again repeated Justice, "The soul that sins must die (Ezek. 18:4). The result of violated law is irrevocable."

Then I saw Mercy advance and enter the tempest. Bending over the wounded being in the same manner as on a former occasion, Mercy said, "Behold! He who *'was and is and is to come'* (Rev. 4:8) descends to earth. By the incarnation of the Spirit, He will renew men to an affinity with the heavenly realms that will exalt them from their fallen condition. By the perfection of His being, He will restore the ruined soul and harmonize the discordant race with eternal law. In Him will be perfected the reunion that will restore the lost planet. Behold the Ransom."

"The Offering is presented," said Justice. "It is in the law of existence, accepted in the law of grace, that He will tread the winepress alone (Isa. 63:3). Yet these angelic hosts seek to rescue the Offering and prevent the consummation."

Then said Mercy to the astonished millions, "It is right that Christ should suffer. Witness the effects of sin upon the sinner's awareness and consciousness of right. The conflict heightens, and the Son of

Man will engage in warfare with the powers of death." Then the multitude said, "Permit us to not witness the scene. Who can endure it?"

"No," said Justice. "Should not the heavens behold and wonder, and should not hell recoil beneath the awful footfall as the God-man proceeds to enter the gate of death, conquer the Enemy of man, and bring *life and immortality to light* (2 Tim. 1:10)?"

"Amen," answered all who saw and heard. "Even so, let Your will, Eternal Spirit, be done in heaven and earth, now and forevermore. Amen."

"Even so, let all heaven respond," said Justice, "that God will be all and over all (1 Cor. 15:28), now and forever."

"Amen! Hallelujah! Hallelujah! Amen!" answered the meek observers of the scene. "Evermore Your will be done! Amen."

Apollyon

As the voices ceased, a view of the conspiracy against the Lamb of God arose as from a smoking pit and appeared above the mass of exasperated mortals in the form of a demon of gigantic dimensions— Apollyon. Upon his head were many horns, each of which emitted an intense flame that, like a cloud, enveloped that portion of the earth in a burning, fiendish hate. Upon his forehead were written the words *Crucify Him! Crucify Him, for He is not worthy to live. He is a seducer of the people.* Upon his breast was written *Apollyon, the Manifestation of Enmity to Good.* Upon his heart was seen in blazing characters the following: *Jesus will not triumph, but death will*

*doom Him to the tomb where mortals slumber and in-
activity reigns. There, He who has called Himself the
Son of God and made Himself equal with God will feel
the death-fetters of my irrevocable decree. Then I will
dash His followers upon the rocks of human prejudice.
Gloom, oppression, and dismay will be their lot
throughout all ages.*

"Hear this," said a sepulchral voice. "Hear this,"
hissed ten thousand serpent-tongued devilish faces,
while the vault below quivered as if some mighty
ruler of a lower region had, with his blazing scepter,
touched the fountain of the mighty deep.

Then out of the pit arose a flame that, although
concealed from mortals, ascended amid this crowd of
devils and caused the sphere of their existence to
blend and burn like mingling flames. Each being appeared to be a self-supporter of the fiery element, so
that the intensity was increased until the host presented the appearance of a burning, destructive
tempest. This pervaded the congregation of mortals,
who were earthly instruments inspired to complete
the merciless and fiendish plan against Jesus, the
meek and humble Sufferer.

"The battle heightens," said an angel, who stood
above the tempest in the atmosphere of heavenly
purity. "With wonder, all the heavens behold the
scene. Now death and hell combine; the powers of
evil charge upon the God-man, who is weighed down
with the sorrows and sins of men."

Another voice asked, "Who will settle the conflict? Myriads of the servants of evil congregate, and
mortals who surround the Sufferer are becoming
like those who inspire them."

Caught Up into Heaven

The Tribunal

Then I saw Jesus being led into the audience chamber of the rulers of the people. Upon His head was a woven crown of thorns. His temples were pierced, and blood ran down His cheeks. His hands were also bound. He did not complain, but looking upward He moved His lips as if speaking. Suddenly the host that had arisen from the pit fell back as though smitten by some mighty hand and exclaimed, "Listen! He speaks with God, and with pity He beholds the multitude of those who mock Him! The conflict is not equal. Our motivation is hate, malice, revenge; His is love, meekness, and submission. We must flee from the power of that gentle Spirit. It is the deepest hell to endure His tenderness, and we cannot contend with His love."

Then Apollyon, the chief manifestation of evil, reappeared in gigantic form. He stretched forth his hand, from which proceeded a dark volume of self-consuming elements. In a voice of terror he said, "Arise! Enter the combat, for now the battle is set! Though Jesus looks upon His tormentors in love, I have turned many hearts of love into hate, many calm spirits into madness, many a praying soul into the utterance of blasphemy. He will not prevail, for now the conflict approaches its completion. This day, by my own hand, I will achieve for myself immortal victory." Having said this, he prompted a mortal to approach Jesus as He stood among His accusers and to strike Him with his hand.

Then I heard a movement as if the heavens above had fallen. I looked, and I saw that all the angels were on their knees, bowing their heads and raising their snow-white and spotless hands toward heaven. Heaven was in mourning.

I saw a mortal approach Jesus, saying, "Are You the Christ? *'Are You the King of the Jews?'* (Matt. 27:11)." Jesus answered, *"It is as you say"* (v. 11). Then the power of darkness gave way, for His voice disturbed the regions of death, and all was silent.

"He, your Redeemer," said Justice to the infants in grief, "is smitten by the impious agent of the sphere of death, and His temples are pierced by the crown of thorns. By this, evil is represented. It is evil's determination to smite the manifestation of good. These vile beings that arise from their lower abode and, like a cloud from some smoking pit, darken the earth are the same evil spirits that torment the sons of men. Filled with lust and unable to indulge the propensity, they seek to vent their gluttonous passions in vengeance upon bewildered mortals. As Jesus will rescue the humble soul from their power; as He is the manifestation of the Incarnate Spirit; and as His mission with men is to sever the power of the Enchanter and break in pieces his kingdom that is established with men; so the prince of the power of darkness will seek to conquer Him and to dash in pieces, like broken pottery, the kingdom of peace that Christ will establish on earth.

"Here the two armies meet. Death and hell arise from the lower armory. Raging with the inextinguishable fires of pride and fiendish hate, being convinced that the decisive hour is at hand, and prompted by Satan, the Deceiver, they venture into battle. The theater of action is the external world.

"The condition of men makes them susceptible to influences of both good and evil. Indeed, humans are intellectual and responsible moral beings. Therefore, they are condemned in their transgressions, and the righteousness of God's throne is set against the sinner. Justice—and Justice is my name—must be maintained even if the violator lives. Man must perish, or through some wise provision there must be a mediator between him and the violated law. For this purpose, a Ransom has been offered, embodying all that is necessary to enter the great vortex of human degradation, grasp the awful current, and stand amid the conflicting elements while rescuing the sinner.

"This can only be brought about by the reversal of the destructive tendency of men. Those arising from the pit unite this deadly tendency with the powers of death and hell. Therefore, to save the sinner, death and hell will be held subject to the will of the Conqueror. The principle of evil will be bound by omnipotent and eternal Will. Mercy has appeared for the depraved race, and in her arms she brings a Ransom, saying that God has given help to Him (Ps. 89:19) and that He is mighty and able to save (Heb. 7:25). Behold! The Offering now descends the vortex."

Then said a voice, "I am Mercy. I offer the Ransom."

Justice replied, "If He is able, He will triumph over death, hell, and the grave; but He will not strive or cry (Matt. 12:19), nor will His voice be heard in contention."

Then answered Mercy, "He is like a lamb for the slaughter. Like a sheep dumb before her shearers, He does not open His mouth." (See Isaiah 53:7.)

"Even so," said Justice, "He will also make His soul an offering for sin before He will see His seed." (See verse 10.)

Again Mercy answered, "Although He descends the vortex of death, His days will be prolonged and the pleasure of the Lord, the work of redemption, will prosper in His hands. (See verse 10.) His kingdom will be an everlasting kingdom (Ps. 145:13), and to His government there will be no end (Isa. 9:7); for through the Mediator, God will be just in the salvation and justification of all who believe."

"Amen!" answered Justice. "Hallelujah, hallelujah, amen!" arose from spirits, angels, and seraphim.

Then I heard Jesus speak to him who had inquired about the nature and purpose of His mission and who had referred Him to the danger of His position. He said, "For this cause I came into the world, that the world might be saved (John 18:37); and since no man can come to the Father but by Me (John 14:6), I submit to the consequence of My mission."

Then with great emotion, Mercy lifted her eyes to the heaven above and said, "Great is Your goodness, O God, since for the salvation of the sinner the just entered death's dominion and rescued the unjust." (See 1 Peter 3:18.) Then approaching Justice, Mercy extended her hand, saying, "Do you accept the Offering I bring as adequate?" Then Justice bowed over the bleeding form of humanity and received the extended hand of Mercy, saying, "When this Offering will have in meekness endured to the end, then the sinner will be restored through repentance toward God and faith in the Lord Jesus."

chapter 15

The Dream of
Pilate's Wife

✤

T hen I saw a company of angels descending from a celestial band far above the scene. As if they were on some errand of mercy where momentous consequences were pending, they proceeded immediately to a palace in the city and paused above it. One of them entered a room in which there was a lovely female whose mind was disturbed by the scene that had moved the exasperated populace. This woman could not see the angel who began to soothe her nervousness and to induce a soft and gentle slumber. "That weary, agitated form," I thought, "has so soon found rest and tranquility under the influence of an angelic being. How free from exciting and disturbing care are the inhabitants of the blissful skies!" She rested, and an angel breathed upon her the breath of pure angelic love.

The female awoke in the spirit and dreamed (as mortals call it) that she stood by a gentle river adorned with the floral beauties of a celestial paradise. The waters of the river were bright and transparent; on their surface was mirrored the transcending beauty of the paradisical landscapes that skirted that living stream and surrounded its pathway. The waters echoed the soft notes of the feathered choirs that rested in the branches of the immortal trees and floated in the spiritual atmosphere above the floral plains.

Charmed to ecstatic delight, the girl lifted her hands as if in adoration. As she raised her eyes, she beheld innumerable inhabitants of the blissful abode, who had just paused in a song of angelic love. The melody of this song reverberated in the holy skies and awoke the hearing of this enraptured dreamer. As she stood beholding the angels above her, she became conscious that the song of the immortal inhabitants had ceased and that the melody of the paradisical birds had died upon the ear. A deathlike stillness held the whole realm in an awful suspense.

While the girl was seeking the cause of this, the scene changed. Gloom veiled the beautiful river. The floral inhabitants folded their leaves and dropped their aroma in the form of tears. The forests stood still; not a leaf moved, for even the celestial breezes paused. The angelic hosts above had veiled their faces. A pale light, as if the image of sadness, occupied the place of the bright glory that had illuminated the world around the girl. Her heart grew faint, her hands fell lifelessly by her side, and her head drooped upon her chest. With her face pale and the image of utter sadness, she looked downward. Her eyes gave up their brilliancy, and life seemed to depart, when an angel touched her, saying, "Pilgrim, why do you wonder? Are you not of the city of Jerusalem, in the land of shadows and of night?"

The dreamer, startled by the voice of the strange speaker, raised her head and saw before her one of the immortal inhabitants clothed in mourning. Surprised, she sought at first to escape, but the angel continued, saying, "Fear not, for no harm will befall you in this land. I come as a messenger from the innumerable company of angels that you saw above you. My errand is one of mercy. You have witnessed the glory, harmony, and melody of this divine abode. Such is the true state of the pure and ever blessed ones. They exist in divine goodness. These rivers, fountains, streams, blossoms, and all living things unite in one expression of ceaseless praise. But you have witnessed the change—how vast and how sudden! You, too, are sad and want to know the cause.

"For this reason I come to you. We suffer with our Lord, who in your city is this day arraigned before a depraved, vindictive, and mock tribunal. Our Lord who suffers there is God manifested in flesh in the person of Jesus. The Jews seek to crucify Him. He goes *"as a lamb to the slaughter"* (Isa 53:7), but woe to those who are His false accusers, vile blasphemers, and unjust prosecutors!

"Spirit of the lost world, you are interested in this trial because of your husband, Pilate. Though he is aware of the innocence of Jesus, he barters innocent blood for the people. Go quickly to him, fall before him, and warn him of his danger. Tell him what you see—how the land of immortality mourns. Tell him that every tree, plant, and flower of that magnificent land now bows in sorrow; that the birds of paradise fold their wings and wait in awful suspense; that the rivers, the transparent waters, wear a heavy gloom that veils their glory; and that angels lay down their crowns, drop their harps, are mute, and fall down in sadness. Meanwhile, Jesus your Redeemer stands before the heartless council of devilish men. Go; do not wait, lest a moment lost may doom Pilate, whom you seek to save."

"Awake!" said the angel who had soothed her to silent slumber. She arose quickly, startled, indeed, terrified by her vision, and hurriedly sent a messenger to tell Pilate her husband, *"Have nothing to do with that just Man, for I have suffered many things today in a dream because of Him"* (Matt. 27:19). But Pilate, disregarding her entreaties, yielded to the insane demands of the people, condemned Jesus to the cross, and gave Him up to be scourged and then crucified.

chapter 16

Jesus Led Away
to Be Crucified

❧

As the sentence was passed and Jesus was being led away to be scourged, the veil that had briefly concealed from our view the inhabitants of the regions of death was removed. Again the Arch-demon and his hosts appeared. He raised his hand, from which a broad sheet of hellish flame came forth and flashed like a banner over the vaults below. Upon it were the words *Victory to Apollyon. This day have I prevailed with men, and they have condemned the Innocent.* Then I heard ten thousand hoarse, hollow voices saying, "Hail, you Prince of Darkness, all hail! You have prevailed, and man will feel the sting of death. Go up to victory! Go up, for we arise from our lower abode and will witness the God-man as He writhes beneath the scorpion lash and agonizes on the Roman cross."

"Aha! Aha!" arose in swelling volume from the fiendish abodes below. The air was pierced by loud shouts uniting with the hellish chant from the mad crowd that rushed to the scene of cruelty.

"Is it not enough?" cried a voice in deep lamentation. "O Justice, are you unrelenting? Is not the Ransom enough? Must we endure this scene? Will the Innocent One continue to suffer at the hands of sinners? Spare Him! His back is torn with lashes!

His temples bleed! His body trembles beneath the heavy burden! He groans in spirit! Must the power of evil prevail? Satan and his legions shout in devilish jubilee over the victory—the victory that condemns Jesus the Innocent to the hands of sinners, to the crown of thorns, to the lash, and to the ignominious and rugged cross, the agent of the cruelest inflictions! Mourn, all you heavens!"

Then Justice answered, "He enters into suffering with the fallen race and endures until the appointed time. His life is not taken, but He gives it for many (John 10:17-18). Although Satan triumphs for a season, the *'strong man, fully armed'* (Luke 11:21) will enter his abode."

Another voice began to cry out, "Arise, you Conqueror, arise and set the captives free! Make bare Your arm and save!" (See Isaiah 52:10.) Still another shouted, "Spare Him the cruel scourging!" Again all the angelic bands, the infants, and their guardians in paradise veiled their faces, and silence prevailed.

The mournful silence of the moment could not fail to deeply impress the great truth intended by the scene upon all who witnessed it. No one could refrain from the deepest and most affecting meditations upon it. The suspense continued until every being was absorbed and pervaded by its influence.

Again Jesus stood before us. His form was disfigured, and He was weak and faint. Still His accusers placed upon His mangled back the huge agent of His execution and forced Him along amid the shouts, jeers, and blasphemies of the people toward the place of crucifixion.

Until this time, I had been made silent by the awfulness of the scenes that were rapidly passing before me. But as Jesus trembled and reeled beneath His load, while His body was bleeding from the cruel scourging, while His temples were gored and swollen from the effects of the crown of thorns, and while the maddening cry, *"Away with Him, away with Him! Crucify Him!"* (John 19:15) rolled over the city, I could endure no longer. I exclaimed to my guide, "Why will Justice not spare the innocent and let the guilty suffer? Let the world endure the consequence of violated law, but do not let innocence endure the pain and woe necessary to unite the sinner with his salvation. Why does this scene continue? Why must Jesus bear the cross? Why are these foolish humans permitted to inflict pain on the pure, even on Him who seeks their good?"

Still Jesus moved slowly along, ready to fall, faint, weary, and in agony. He spoke no words but looked with love and pity upon His tormentors. While I was reasoning and wondering, I discovered that He moved more unsteadily, less firmly even than before, until He sank down beneath His burden. His humanity had failed, and as He yielded from His spirit within Him, He groaned, and all was still.

For the first time, His persecutors and crucifiers paused in their cruelty and showed care for Him. I thought that perhaps this care was on account of fear that they would not enjoy the benefits of His prolonged suffering upon the cross, beneath which He now lay bleeding. As He fell, the effect on the saints and angels was beyond any power to describe. Truly it appeared that the heavens themselves would fail and happiness would depart so as never to be restored.

The scene had been increasing in its awfulness, but when Jesus yielded beneath the heavy load and the continued scourging, all the spirits moved as if they gladly would have relieved Him. At this point, a voice uttered from afar, "It is written of Him that He treads the winepress alone." (See Isaiah 63:3.)

Justice said, "Let the inhabitants of earth and the angels of heaven know that He endures for sinners. By His stripes they are healed (Isa. 53:5). He enters the gate of death so that He may rescue those who have fallen by transgression."

"Amen," answered Mercy, who now appeared above the cross. "Indeed, He offered Himself for sinners. Justice, here is the Offering I bring."

"You have said," replied Justice, "that He suffers. He does not suffer from any vindictive wrath inflicted from the Father of Life, but He suffers from the consequences of a law that has been violated by those whom He seeks to rescue. The hearts He seeks to save have been made malicious by evil inspiration. It is the nature of sin to seek to destroy good. Sin, if uncontrolled, would blot out the sun, make the heavens a pandemonium of evil and malicious beings, break in pieces the government of the Lord Creator, and render void the moral principles and the nature of the heavens full of angelic beings. It would demolish God's throne and destroy eternal things.

"Sin is the opposite of good; it knows no sympathy and is a fountain of malicious intentions. Thus, when Jesus appears as a ransom for the sinner and enters into sympathy with those who have violated the law of being, they, controlled by the principles of evil, seek to torture and destroy Him, although He is the messenger of peace and goodwill to them.

"Before you who are assembled, the nature and workings of the principles of good and evil are made to appear. The Arch-deceiver, Apollyon, is the concentrated embodiment of the nature and forces of evil. Demoniacal beings, because of their obedience to Apollyon, have a great affinity with him. They have gathered together above those excited mortals on earth like a cloud of smoke and blackness, and they are about to inspire with evil the deluded and enthusiastic mortals who, like a tempest, are driven by the interior force. These mortals are seekers and lovers of the ways of evil to various degrees. Therefore, they are the willing subjects of the wicked plan. Hence, they meet on the earthly plain of action, and with them a union of envious desire prevails.

"Jesus of Nazareth, God manifested in flesh, is the manifestation of goodness itself—divine good, harmonic existence, universal love, and paternal care. *'In Him dwells all the fullness of the Godhead'* (Col. 2:9), the attributes of divine existence, divine life, and universal good. Men who are fallen are the occupants of earth, the intermediate place; immortal demons are not its occupants. Jesus seeks to save men's souls, and demons seek to destroy them. Jesus entered their abode as their Redeemer, while Apollyon approaches to destroy. With these two principles, there can be no union; therefore, Jesus does not suffer by heaven's decree but by reason of His goodness, His mission for the sinner, and His entrance into the scene of combat with death and hell."

"Will He prevail?" inquired an angel who had listened to this address of Justice.

"Yes," uttered Mercy, "He will prevail. He is *'the Lion of the tribe of Judah'* (Rev. 5:5), *'the Bright and Morning Star'* (Rev. 22:16). He will prevail and will unloose the seals (Rev. 5:2–5)."

"Alleluia! Alleluia! He will prevail," arose from the myriads congregated. *"Your kingdom come. Your will be done on earth as it is in heaven"* (Matt. 6:10).

"Even so, amen!" said Justice, and again silence prevailed.

No movement or voice disturbed the spellbound atmosphere while Justice and Mercy paused, for it appeared that all who witnessed the scene—even the wicked on earth, those from spheres of darkness among the regions of the dead, and those from lower abodes where evil reigns—felt the innocence of Jesus the meek Sufferer. Surely it could not have been otherwise when His true character was considered. No fault could be found in Him, in His life, when He was betrayed, or when He was condemned to the cross.

This is the only proper conclusion when one remembers that He had been betrayed (Matt. 26:47–50), had been arrayed in mock royalty before Herod (Luke 23:11), and had endured the cruel and false accusations of the priests. His temples had been pierced with thorns, and His back had been lacerated with severe scourging, yet He had not opened His mouth in complaint. (See Acts 8:32.) In perfect honesty, He had replied to interrogations, though it seemed that His destiny depended on the answers He gave. No evasion of truth had stained His holy lips. Finally, in all things He had honored His high claims to divinity and had established His nature in righteousness.

In His life, He had walked among men as a benefactor. He had healed the sick, raised the dead, and cast out evil spirits, restoring tranquility and happiness to those who were grievously tormented by them. He had bound up the brokenhearted and caused the mourner to rejoice. He had forgiven transgressors and filled their hearts with gladness and heavenly love. He had faithfully reproved the vile and cleansed the temple of money changers. And when He was opposed and persecuted, even condemned to the cross, He did not speak against anyone but, by His meekness and harmony, He had revealed what could only have been divine.

When the cross upon which He was to be executed was laid upon His bleeding shoulders, He had meekly bowed under it and carried it along, amid loud shouts of approval and bitter taunts. Thus He occupied the most humiliating and suffering condition that any man could endure. When he had fallen beneath the cross, exhausted in His humanity by excessive and prolonged suffering, His spirit groaned, but without complaint. Then He looked upon His accusers and tormentors with pity. He remembered their depraved state and felt compassion for them.

Thus the Savior of sinners suffered without any sympathy except that of a few personal friends whose spirits agonized with Him but had no means to offer aid. Jesus bled, groaned, fainted, and fell, but no tear stole down the hardened cheek of the cruel, mocking Jews. No soft hand gently touched His wounded temples. No words of consolation were spoken to Him. Alone He endured, alone He bled, alone He struggled to bear the cross.

How could those who witnessed His suffering fail to sympathize with Him? How could mortals hold back their tears? How could anyone fail to love

One so excellent? How could they prevent their souls from adoring One so worthy, especially since He suffered, not only innocently, but also for their salvation?

Finally, the soldiers commanded Jesus to arise and proceed to Calvary. Obedient, He struggled beneath the cross, but His trembling limbs failed, and again He sank back in His agony. Who can depict the scene? What artist, with pencil formed of immortal colors, could so touch the senses of man and blend the light and shadows with skill sufficient to reveal the great reality of the scene?

There was the Savior—the spotless, holy, and lovely Jesus—struggling with convulsive effort under the scourger's lash to raise the cross beneath which He had fallen. Blood from His bleeding body stained the ground. His severed flesh quivered from repeated strokes of the vigorous whip. His swollen face was more marred than any man's. His eyes of love were concealed beneath blood and tears. His holy lips moved, prompted by His heart, which was ever full of love and pity, and they said, "Sinner, for you I freely suffer; for you I endure these afflictions. Yes, I endure them so that you may be saved."

After repeated, ineffective efforts to force Jesus to bear His cross alone, the people were anxious to revel in His sufferings during the final ordeal. Orders were given to the soldiers, who compelled Simon of Cyrene to bear the cross (Matt. 27:32). And again they proceeded.

As they advanced slowly toward Calvary, a group of women approached the dictators of the awful tragedy. Bowing before them, the women raised their hands and, in a most affecting manner, pleaded that Jesus should be released. No attitude could better correspond with the object of their prayer. Their sorrow was inexpressible; their cause was just; their petition humble and urgent, but all to no avail. "He will perish," said the proud priests, and again the multitude shouted, "Crucify Him! Crucify Him! Test His power. If He is the Son of God, let Him break the arm of strength that moves Him toward Calvary, where His weakness, foolishness, and blasphemy will be revealed."

"No," said the humble petitioners, "spare Him, for our sake. Are we not your sisters? Do we not love you, our brethren? Hear us. Let our petition be regarded. Let woman's love prevail. You do not know Him. His heart is full of love for all. His soul is one of pity and tenderness. We love you no less, though we also love Jesus. His goodness has won our hearts. We plead His cause. Save Him. His feeble limbs fail; He falls beneath the load. Can you not spare Him? Oh, remember and regard us! Remember the love of faithful woman, her tenderness and faithfulness in the hour of trial. Then remember Jesus for whom we plead."

"Never!" answered a haughty high priest coldly and sternly. "He deserves death. He will be crucified."

"He will be crucified," shouted the multitude, and the group of mediators sank down in despair.

chapter 17

Judas's Remorse

❦

Before us was now displayed the Jewish Sanhedrin. They were expressing many thanks for the triumph of truth over error, and of good sense over fanaticism. They congratulated each other in the hope of peace that must result from the prompt and efficient action taken to put down Jesus, whom they saw as an impostor.

Their general appearance revealed a proud, tyrannical spirit rather than that of God's humble servants. There was more frivolity displayed than religion, more Pharisaism than meekness, more lordship than ministry. While they were reveling in the glow of their triumphant feelings, Judas, now the picture of wretchedness, rushed into their midst and wildly exclaimed, *"'I have sinned by betraying innocent blood.' And they said* [to him], *'What is that to us? You see to it!'"* (Matt. 27:4).

At this cold reply, Judas was startled. He had expected their sympathy and aid in his trial. Having served them, he had gone to them for help, and their indignity toward him only added sorrow to sorrow, disappointment to disappointment, remorse to remorse, and despair to wretchedness. Recovering partially from the shock produced by the unexpected reply, he said, "In this hour of trouble, should I not expect sympathy from those who pledged honor, blessing, and friendship to whoever would conduct them to the capture of Jesus? Did I not faithfully fulfill my promise and give Him into the hands of soldiers? Why, then, this cold and indifferent reply? For you I betrayed my innocent Master; for you I hailed Him in my accustomed and confident manner. Moreover, for you I sealed my treachery with a kiss. Will I not now find you as faithful to your most solemn pledge?"

Then, looking down as if in deep and painful thought, he exclaimed, "When I betrayed Him, He looked upon me in love. I can still see that look. I feel its power. He was just and good. I have betrayed innocent blood." Hastily throwing down the silver for which he had bartered Jesus, he said, "Here is the price of my Lord and my peace forever."

Then answered a priest, "True, that is the price. We purchased your services for that amount. Why trouble us? Take it; it is yours. We have no more need of you. Our purpose in you has been accomplished. Leave here, before you suffer the same fate as your Master. By complaining to us, you imply that Jesus, the outlaw, is our King. Get out, lest the guards bear you to Calvary, too."

The Depravity of Man

Then a mighty angel drew near, saying, "Consider the procedures of men revealed in the case of Judas, the chief priests, and the rulers of the Jews. They have followed the natural promptings of the depraved heart. May it not then be truly said that *'the carnal mind is enmity against God; for it is not*

subject to the law of God, nor indeed can be' (Rom.
8:7)? *'God is light and in Him is no darkness'* (1
John 1:5). God is just; His ways are ways of righteousness. God is good; with love and paternal care
He looks upon the workmanship of His hands. God is
faithful and true (Rev. 19:11); His Word endures forever (1 Pet. 1:25). His promises are Yes and Amen (2
Cor. 1:20).

"Are not the ways of man the opposite? Are they
not too often designed in selfishness and carried out
in secrecy? Are not the tendencies of man's pro-
ceedings unrighteous? Does he not seek his own and
not another's welfare? Is man faithful to what is
right? Does he abide in confidence and keep his
pledge? Indeed, does he not proceed for selfish ends?
Even though he has made promises, does he not too
often break them when his purposes and interests
dictate?

"Inquire of Earth. Let her ages, buried in the
past, relate the history and thus reveal the nature of
the human heart. Let the wise man, the philosopher,
and the poet give a faithful answer. Awake from
their silent repose those who slumber in the tombs!
Let lords, rulers, and priests speak from their high
positions, and all will reveal the truth that man is
depraved. Let the tears and sorrows of the servant
and the slave unite, and they will relate the sad
story of human woe, whose source is found alone in
the perversion of the heart of man.

"Judas betrayed his Lord by bartering justice
and goodness for mammon. (See Matthew 6:24.) His
actions have been revealed, but they are only the ex-
treme degree of the depravity that exists within all
unsanctified desires. He sacrificed his greater good,

his Best Friend, for applause and gain. Does not man often proceed along these lines? Does he not often barter friendship and forsake his brother, leaving him to struggle amid accumulating sorrows? Though earth's philosophers gladly would conceal the horrid picture, does not man betray his fellowman for present gain?

"In heaven there are no false ones. No sanctified spirit barters another spirit into bondage; none commits a companion to disgrace and death in order to gain money or fame. Indeed, let the angels repeat it. An angel could never betray another angel for anything that the universe bestows, nor would he forsake him in the hour of trial. Never! There is no Judas in the world of light," continued the angel. "No likeness of fallen man exists on high. How, then, can man's heart itself rise to angelic life while it is still unchanged?"

Then said another angel, who approached from an opposite direction, "May not these truths be revealed to the infants' understanding?"

Immediately a scene was before us in which Earth, with her various movements, was displayed. In this scene, brothers were betraying brothers for gain; parents, their children; husbands, their wives. Friends were exchanging each other as mere commodities, nations were in their wars and piracy, and the poor and dependent were grievously afflicted. Multitudes of human beings were seen suffering in lowest degradation, living and dying without hope.

Mothers were convulsively pressing their babes to their hearts for the last time and imprinting on their rosy lips a farewell kiss, while the young ones clung with dying hold to their mothers' necks. Husbands were looking in despair upon their maltreated wives and heartbroken children. Poverty, oppression, pain, anguish, plunder, and murder were revealed.

In the midst of these mixed multitudes were a few who were striving to unloose the fetters of those bound; to take from the scourger his cruel implements; to provide means for the sufferings of every class; to feed the hungry, clothe the naked, bind up the brokenhearted; to change war into peace; to make the battlefield a school for the fostering of the poor and dependent; to cultivate true friendship and promote true religion; to enlighten the bigot; to prevent persecution; and to establish universal liberty and harmony, founded upon justice and mercy. But their encouragement was limited. Still, they did not fail to be ever engaged in deeds of benevolence.

As we were observing this scene, an angel said, "Will you instruct the infants concerning the cause of this strange perversion and why these philanthropists do not faint in the toil, seeing that they have so little sympathy from those for whose benefit they labor so ardently?"

"Let Earth provide the answer," said the angel. "The ways of men reveal the perversion of their hearts. Heaven can reveal the cause. Heaven can also tell you why those messengers of mercy, those who mingle with the sons of men to seek their salvation, do not faint."

God's Love Reaches Out to Man

Then a light descended, and over each of those who were engaged in the work of rescue was a guardian angel who, appointed by heaven and full of the Holy Spirit, sought to encourage each of them in their labors and to impress them with holy and benevolent desires. Another light also descended from some invisible source and pervaded the heart of each mortal who, in the name of the cross, was struggling to lead the forlorn race.

"This," said the angel, "is holy inspiration. The Spirit of God inspires all who are born of God, so that they may labor continually for man's restoration from sin and from its consequent misery, and for man's final exaltation to a state of bliss.

"But," continued the angel, "nothing can reveal to human understanding the depth of degradation of a heart that can be accessory to such deeds of cruelty as have been presented here. Although angels behold with wonder the acts and unfaithfulness of men, they are common to man and natural to his perverted being. In fact, they are so common that man not only witnesses them without regret, but he may also be persuaded to engage in them in exchange for money. To redeem man requires goodness beyond finite comprehension. No one but God, who is Love and who is mighty and able to save (see Hebrews 7:25), could rescue the fallen race."

Then the angels said, "Let all in heaven raise their voices in praises high and holy, *'for God so loved the world that He gave His only begotten Son, that whoever believes in Him should* [obtain salvation]*'* (John 3:16)."

"Yes, we will adore our God for the manifestation of His love to man, who is dead in trespasses and sin" (see Ephesians 2:1), answered the attending angels. "He has given help to One who is mighty and

able to save. (See Psalm 89:19.) We will praise Him;
we will praise Him evermore. Amen."

"Surely," continued the speaker, "He waives His
high privileges in order to exalt the ruined planet, to
harmonize the discordant race, and to save the deceived spirits of men. He permits human hearts to
reveal their hidden natures. In this, God is just, for
heaven witnesses and, while beholding, pities them.
The angels who are commissioned, as ministering
spirits, to seek the souls of men take delight in doing
so. Indeed, they delight to visit earth on errands of
mercy."

"Angels delight to do the will of God evermore,"
repeated the vast assembly as the scene changed.

"Rest," said the chief guardian, "you infant observers. For a season, mingle in the social scenes of
paradisical enjoyment."

Then addressing a company of spirits to the
right, the angel said, "Bring the flowers gathered
upon the holy plains. Let every infant spirit be re-
freshed. Let the fragrance from the floral mountain
descend, and let joy possess each spirit. Spirit of holy
quiet, pervade them with your everlasting peace."

The entertainment that followed was perfectly
adapted to the need for quieting one's mind after so
much excitement over subjects so thrilling and vast.
Angels from the superior spheres mingled in all sim-
plicity with the saints, guardians, and infants.

Familiar sentiment was continually chanted by
groups who were in different sections of the temple.
Visitors from the plains adorned the temple with
clusters of flowers. Maidens placed wreaths of flowers of many colors around the infants' heads, whose
golden locks reflected beauty mingling with the

harmoniously combined prismatic hues. Youths who accompanied the maidens from the plains waved palm branches gathered from the delightful groves. Finally, the infants were presented with golden goblets from which they sipped as from fountains of living waters. They also partook of fruit gathered from immortal trees—the fruit of paradise. On each of their hands, there hovered a bird of many colors, whose warbling notes had charmed their senses.

Then I heard a voice saying, "Who could fail to praise God for existence, for immortality, and for the bliss of paradise?" The infants caught the sound and understood the sentiment. Raising their hands, they replied, "We will adore our heavenly Father. We will always mention with love and reverence the name of our Redeemer. We will cheerfully be led and conducted by our guardian angels. And when we have been prepared and our understanding has been properly enlightened, we will go forth as servants of goodness, wherever the Lord our Redeemer will direct.

"In deeds of usefulness as well as with our voices, and upon stringed instruments, we will praise and adore the Lord Most High. We will learn wisdom as heaven reveals it to us."

"Amen," answered the guardian spirits. "For this we delight to instruct your youthful intellects and teach your spirits to worship the Lord. For this exalted occupation, we will unite in anthems to God forevermore." Then each guardian moved her hand as a sign of a change, and all were soon in their former position.

chapter 18

Calvary

❧

T hen a voice full of sympathy spoke from a
cloud that rested far above, saying, "Calvary
reveals her wonders. Prepare to witness the
last struggle of the Redeemer as He meets Death,
the destroyer."

As this voice ceased, the chief guardian raised
her eyes and holy hands, saying, "O Lord our Pre-
server, bestow supporting aid upon us. Preserve our
minds while we witness this scene. Prepare us to
understand. Pervade us with meekness, reverence,
and holy love.

"Around this scene," continued the voice,
"gather interests as lasting as immortality, as momentous as the worth of undying spirits. Let the sun
be darkened and the stars be veiled. Let nature
pause and heaven be silent. You seraphim and
cherubim, while the scene transpires, lay down your
celestial instruments, upon which you utter holy anthems. You floral universes, droop your heads. You
waters, stand still, and do not let the rippling murmur break the silence. You birds who warble in immortal groves, be mute. Pause, you breezes, while
the Redeemer suffers."

Then, beneath pale shadows, appeared Calvary.
I could perceive a crowd of people who were apparently transfixed. In the center were three crosses on

which human forms were hanging. Near them was a band of soldiers, seated as if they had been engaged in gambling, but they, too, seemed stunned from some unexpected cause.

Mournful murmurings were heard as though at a great distance. These murmurings seemed to still the very spirit of life in all. A feeling of gloom, approaching utter despair, was visible on the face of every spirit.

At length a low whisper passed from guardian to guardian: "Listen! Nature breathes a solemn requiem! Nature suffers. Alas!" Again all was still. No sound or movement disturbed the silent gloom.

Gradually a pale light shone over Calvary, revealing the scene more clearly. The three crosses became more visible, until the form and features of the sufferers were plainly distinguished.

"It is Jesus! Jesus suffers! Jesus is dying!" burst from every spirit. A sudden shuddering seized them, and they bowed their faces, still repeating, "Jesus suffers! Jesus is dying!"

While they were thus bowing, Jesus said, *"Father, forgive them, for they do not know what they do"* (Luke 23:34).

"Oh, what love, what wonderful goodness!" acknowledged the humble spirits. "He prays for His crucifiers. Give us, O Supreme God, the essence of that spirit evermore."

While Jesus prayed, the soldiers and the rulers derided Him, saying, *"He saved others; let Him save Himself if He is the Christ, the chosen of God"* (v. 35). This cold and cruel taunt caused the spirits to raise their heads and look steadfastly upon the scene. But their sympathy and sorrow can never be revealed.

Calvary

Near the cross, a few of the friends of Jesus were bowing. Their excess of sorrow had brought them past weeping. Agony held them even as death holds a pale corpse. One of these friends was Mary, the mother of Jesus, who had ever lingered near Him during His sufferings but who appeared conscious of the certainty of His trial. She suffered with Him but could not save Him.

Jesus, turning His eye upon the group, said to Mary, *"Woman, behold your son!"* (John 19:26). Then addressing the Beloved Disciple, John, He said, *"Behold your mother!"* (v. 27). And so, in His agony, He displayed His humanity and invited the disciple to support Mary, who was sinking beneath her weight of grief. The disciple then supported Mary, who leaned upon him as she looked upon her Son in His last trial.

Then one of the criminals who was crucified with Jesus railed against Him, saying, *"If You are the Christ, save Yourself and us"* (Luke 23:39). To this the Lord made no reply but looked in pity upon him. The other criminal rebuked his fellow, saying, *"We receive the due reward of our deeds; but this Man has done nothing wrong"* (v. 41). Then in a devout manner he said to Jesus, "Those who have led You here delight in their foolishness. They vainly suppose that You are conquered and slain. But I feel from you an influence superior to man. You are from everlasting to everlasting. Mystery hangs about you, O Lord! I know that in You exist the fountains of life. You live forevermore. Will you, O Lord, *'remember me when You come into Your kingdom'* (v. 42)?"

Then the Lord looked upon him, and love from His Spirit overshadowed and pervaded the man. The Holy Spirit worked in his heart the change that was necessary for his union with the enduring principles of divine life and love. In answer to his prayer, Jesus said, "Because you have sought help from your heart, your prayer is answered. *'Assuredly, I say to you, today you will be with Me in Paradise'* (Luke 23:43)."

This reply was like life given to the dead. The criminal, although in the agonies of death, manifested the emotion of a soul forgiven and a spirit made free. He was not set free from his earthly execution, but with heaven's pardon, he was given a release from the power of sin and death. He feared no longer. Through Jesus, all heaven had been secured in this last and trying moment. His physical sufferings seemed to charm his body to rest, while his soul shone forth amid the darkness and hovered over the gulf of death, ready for its happy flight. He was ready for his exit from death to life, from mortality to the possession of eternal realities.

While this scene was transpiring, the mockers around the cross had not noticed the divinity of Jesus manifested in the forgiveness of sin. But the angels and infants looked with wonder and gratitude upon the goodness displayed in that trying moment. The impression was so deep that afterwards, whenever the infants would refer to the crucifixion, they would name the thief, speak of his prayer, and mention the benevolent answer of the Redeemer—the answer by which all heaven was given to the dying sinner.

The Last Struggle

Darkness now began to fold more closely around the scene. No sun, moon, or stars were visible. Night in heavy gloom veiled the earth.

While we were witnessing the scene that only revealed cruelty added to cruelty, a terrible form approached Jesus. Around the ghostly face of this form, like satellites, revolved innumerable lesser creatures like him. In broad capital letters, the words *YOU WILL TRIUMPH, YOU TRIUMPHANT KING* were written on the sphere that encompassed him. His appearance was like one sure of victory when engaging in a final conflict. And upon the outcome of this conflict depended the interests of ages.

With a hoarse, sepulchral voice, a voice of terror, and in a manner characteristic of a never failing conqueror, he addressed Jesus, who hung upon the cross: "I arise and meet you in this Your day of folly. You are chained. You are a victim. Angels, saints, and men have shouted Your triumph over death. Death is my name. You have attempted to reverse the law by which I exist—the law that feeds the hungry tombs with the bodies of infants, youths, and the elderly; the law that has moved in might and that none can hinder; the law that this day grapples with You. You will perish. I came to seize this vessel and dash it against the marble rock of dissolution." Then reaching forth his hand, he seized the body of Jesus, whose sensitive nerves quivered from the touch of his cold, contracting fingers.

Then Jesus cried, *"My God, My God, why have You forsaken Me?"* (Mark 15:34). At this, a voice said from above, "He treads the winepress alone." (See Isaiah 63:3.)

"Nevertheless," answered another voice, "He suffers, *'the just for the unjust'* (1 Pet. 3:18)."

"Then I have gotten the victory!" shouted Death. "He who *'was in the beginning with God'* (John 1:2) now enters the destructive elements where violated law breaks the violator into pieces. He enters so that He may rescue, but He will also perish. He fails. Let hell arise and behold. Let all you angelic hosts witness, behold, and wonder while Jesus struggles in my right hand. You have sung through all heaven that He would vanquish Death, but see how He struggles while I hold Him with my might and while I triumph over Him!

"I alone grasp this God-man and leap with Him amid the tombs. Aha! You chant His victory, but you ought to be chanting His defeat! I hold the Conqueror. Move back, you heavens, before I ascend from sphere to sphere, shake the eternal throne, and turn these celestial worlds into a cemetery for the dead." Then with a wild, exultant glare, he met the Savior's face and said with menacing reproach, "How futile for You to seek triumph in this matter! Have I not slain innumerable legions? How can You think about escaping? No, Jesus, You God-man, I sacrifice You, my last foe."

Around this scene had again congregated the hosts of vile spirits. Apollyon led them in his triumph. They were all waving in the infernal breezes their black banners, upon which appeared the images of Apollyon, the embodiment of evil, and Death, the cruel destroyer, embracing each other over the image of the cross and the bleeding Sacrifice. Then followed bold blasphemies, boisterous shouting, and wild, devilish laughter. The messengers of evil moved to and fro like waves of thick, black waters, while their hellish jubilee burst forth as from a compressed sea of madness and fiendish delight.

They moved around Jesus, shouting, "Aha! Aha!" while Death was addressing Him. Their triumph appeared sure.

Apollyon said, "He fails in this decisive hour. Begin your death song, you congregated millions, for Jesus the boasted Son of God is at last subdued! Death prevails!"

Then the divinity of Jesus said, "No man takes My life. I lay it down of Myself (John 10:18). You who seek Me employ men in the external world as agents of slaughter and execution, but they have no power over Me except what is given them. Behold! I come through death's portals to bind you, you destroyer, and to rescue My people from your power—those whom I redeem.

"So that I may prevail, I meet you in your dominions. Behold, I come! You are caught by your own scheme. I do not meet you in vengeance, but to open the tomb and set the captives free, to open the prison door of those bound and imprisoned, and to bind you and destroy your power. I have descended amid dissolving elements, humanity being the chariot in which I enter the dark dominions where mortality fails. You are conquered. The law of life and harmony will entwine your form and establish the boundaries of your dominions. And thus you will await the day when Death and hell will be cast into the bottomless abyss, and they will no more afflict My people."

Having said this, He bound Death with a chain of light.

Then raising His eyes toward Justice, who witnessed from the cloud, He said, "Behold, the Spirit of

Life prevails over death." And addressing the roaring tempest that gathered its mighty maelstrom around Him and broke in fearful whirlpools upon Him, He said, "Hold back, you angry flood! Roll back your waters, you death currents! Unloose your grasp, you boasting conqueror, you prince of terrors! I come to rescue the fallen planet, before it plunges into the bottomless abyss." Then raising His right hand of divine strength while standing in the mighty torrent, He touched a planet that hung upon the brink, ready to plunge. Its millions of inhabitants lay amid surging waves that drove madly down the gulf of death.

While thus holding the suspended planet, Jesus said, "Hold back, you tempest, terrible in might! Although your waves fearfully gather around the fallen world; although your current draws with immensity of strength; although you have forced Earth along the death-surge of ages, be still! Earth, reverse your movement, and arise! The day of your salvation dawns. You mighty winds of heaven, fan into life the expiring planet. You pure waters, ever flowing from life's ceaseless fountains, let your cooling tides move over her parched and barren soil. You angels who minister in love, gather quickly around the discordant race, administer life's stimulating drink, and with truth cure the evil of false and perverted hearts. Bar the gateway to immortal slumbers, so that forlorn man may not enter there. And you, Death," He continued, "although you boast that you have slain millions, upon you I fix My seal. You are bound, and your days are numbered. Hell, your kingdom of mortality, the trophy of victorious ages, will fall. And you, having no more kingdoms to demolish, will die at the appointed time."

Then addressing Apollyon, He said, "You foe of equity, harmony, peace, and heaven, depart quickly to the regions from which you have come. Lead your forces toward your own ruin, for at the appointed time, you, too, will feel restraining power I have come to rescue My people."

Jesus then moved His hand, and Apollyon departed with his legions. Then a dark cloud that accompanied them concealed them from our view.

The Lord then said, *"Father, into Your hands I commit My spirit"* (Luke 23:46), and with a loud voice He cried, *"It is finished!"* (John 19:30). Then holding Death subject to His will, He descended to the spirits in prison. (See 1 Peter 3:18–20.)

The Tomb

The scene of the crucifixion had scarcely passed, when a soft light gently descended, revealing a solitary tomb around which armed guards were stationed. To that tomb the body of Jesus was entrusted. An angel standing nearby touched the tomb with a scepter he held in his right hand, and to us it became transparent, revealing the body in its quiet rest. To behold that body thus at rest was pleasure, for it removed the anxiety caused by witnessing the sufferings of Jesus while He passed through His many cruel trials from the Garden of Gethsemane to Calvary.

Now His body, shrouded in clean linen unstained by blood, calmly rested in the sepulchre. The still and noiseless atmosphere, undisturbed by the clamor of the shouting masses, along with the sweet sleep of that body now in its quiet home, joined together to soothe the minds of those who had been overwhelmed by the former revolting scenes of cruelty and slaughter.

"How calm, how composed the body of Jesus is now!" said the chief guardian, while we were enjoying rest in our spirits as we looked upon it.

"Yes, Jesus rests," answered a voice, and Mercy appeared above the tomb. "Yes, He rests. He makes the tomb His bed. With His people He slumbers in the grave. He sanctified the sepulchre of His saints. But He sleeps only to awaken again. He also will awaken all who sleep in death." (See 1 Corinthians 15:51–53.)

Then one of the celestial choirs descended and chanted over the tomb where Jesus lay: "Peace and quiet slumber, holy rest, fold gently in your gracious arms the body of the Lord, which will never again endure pain. Holy angels, guard the sacred tomb. Let no intruder pass the portals of this temple where the body of the Redeemer rests. Hold back the dissolving elements, so that they will not change it. Do not let it see corruption. (See Acts 2:27.) Do not let worms feed upon it. It has been sanctified through suffering."

Then in loud shouts, another company of angels chanted, "That body will arise again. It will ascend to the highest heaven. It will be the center around which saints will gather. It will attract unto itself, in the realms of immortality, the sanctified dust, the renovated bodies of the saints."

"Let it rest," continued the band of quiet singers. "Be still, you winds that howl around the walls of Jerusalem, be still. As you pass this way, fold your hurried wings, and glide gently by. Jesus, the manifestation of divine good, has no more sorrow. His body slumbers here. Do not touch it, you cold and impure winds of earth. Let heaven fan it with the softest breezes. Let the most sacred harmonies linger around this consecrated tomb."

Again the choir chanted above, "Let the heavens resume their lyres and strike their highest notes to lofty anthems. Jesus will awake and ascend in clouds of glory. Universes will join the song of His ascension. Echo, you everlasting hills, echo His name in triumphant song."

Then the former group continued, "Soft and gentle as the breath of newborn love in the serene heavens, let us sing, 'Here slumbers the body of the Lord.' We will speak His name in softest tones. Jesus, You external manifestation of our Lord, sleep on. Rest, mangled form. Rest in the sacred tomb. We will linger nearby while the tomb retains this precious treasure."

"Fold your arms and hover in the holy atmosphere, all you commissioned ones. Do not let a voice be heard while the body rests," said Mercy to the holy ones attending, as they hovered around the tomb. Language can never reveal that scene or in any way express the sacred peace that pervaded the spirits before whom it was transpiring.

It was joy beyond measure to see the body of Jesus at rest. It was sacred quiet. It was fullness of harmony to listen to the soft anthems of the angels who watched the tomb. Surely it may be said that Jesus sanctified the grave. I can never reflect upon that scene without a desire that my poor body should rest there also. I wish to lay it down in the tomb. The grave no longer seems gloomy to me. Rather, it is the most sacred place of all on earth. There Jesus my Redeemer slumbered. There His body rested. There it was free from pain. Only let me be worthy, and at the appointed time, I will cheerfully step into the grave and lay my body down to rest. There, in peace, it will await the morning of the Resurrection.

chapter 19

The Resurrection

❧

"Behold and wonder, you inhabitants of paradise," said a mighty angel as he descended and stood upon the tomb. "Yes, behold as the Son of Man comes from the abode of desolation. He comes as a conqueror from the regions of the dead."

While he was still speaking, Jesus, even the Incarnate Spirit, the Spirit of Redemption, appeared walking among the tombs. As He looked over them, he said, "Here the bodies of My people sleep. The night of your slumbers has been long and dreary, and the bed on which you have rested has been cold. Massive walls, enclosing this vast arena, have guarded and confined you while you have slept. You are precious dust, since you have been the dwellings of the spirits I redeem. You will arise.

"This darkness that has so long shrouded your abode in night, adding gloom to gloom, will be dispersed by the light of life. I have come to illuminate this dark and solitary vault, this charnel house of the dead; to determine the limits of death and the grave; and to open a door of escape. Sleep on, you sacred relics, dust of My people. Sleep on until you are animated by the quickening, purifying, and exalting principle of eternal law. Sleep on until life from on high will redeem and spiritualize your

169

bodies and prepare them for the immortal and incorruptible habitations of the spirit in its heavenly existence. Sleep on until that day when you are called from this silent slumber to spheres of life. The tomb will be illuminated. From now on, the totality of its darkness will be no more."

Then lifting His eyes, He said, "Watchman from the everlasting hills, descend and enter this abode. Keep guard until the morning of the Resurrection, when I will call you to arise with these ashes—ashes that, once quickened into life, refined, purified, and reorganized, will become the outer garments of My redeemed people. With divine certainty, that day surely comes." Then one who was mighty in strength and whose garment reflected ten thousand interwoven crosses entered the arena from the mountain of light. Addressing Jesus, he said, *"Behold, I have come...to do Your will, O God"* (Heb. 10:7).

The Lord replied, "Guard this tomb where mortality slumbers." Into his right hand the Lord placed a scepter, upon whose burnished shaft was engraved the image of the cross and also, in hieroglyphics, the solemn events of the trial and crucifixion. Jesus said to him, "With this scepter you will defend and control these dominions until heaven calls for you."

The watchman answered, "Be my help. Your will be done evermore."

The divine Spirit then approached a tomb over which angels watched and in which the body of Jesus lay. With a voice that indicated supreme power, He said, "Let life descend upon this inanimate form. Let the quickening Spirit pervade and quicken this body. Let every organ, tissue, and property thereof be transformed into life and be immortalized. Let this body arise."

Then light from the divine Spirit encompassed the body, and a sudden shaking seized the walls and foundations of the tombs.

Death Is Defeated

And the body of Jesus arose, at which time a mighty angel said with a loud voice, "Jesus prevails; He arises triumphant. Death has no power over Him; He breaks the strong bands of Death, and He lives evermore. Raise your anthems high, all you who dwell in worlds of light. Jesus reigns!"

"Hallelujah! Amen! Jesus reigns!" answered the innumerable companies of angels who had witnessed the reanimation and resurrection of the body of Jesus.

Then Justice, who was still observing the scene, said, "Although you shout that He is victorious, He remains with the dead."

Then Jesus approached the massive gate that blocked the opening of the tomb. Reaching forth His hand, He touched its mighty bars, and behold, they crumbled to dust! He then said, "Be unbarred, you mighty gate! Your keeper, even Death, has no more power over you. His limits are determined. Yes, although man has violated the law of life, and although the outer man wastes away (2 Cor. 4:16) and dies as Adam did, even so, by the law of life revealed through the Incarnate Spirit, man will be restored in Jesus; he will live again.

"The grave will not have everlasting dominion over the ashes of the dead, nor will it exist as a perpetual valley of darkness between earth and the regions occupied by those spirits who have departed from the outer world."

Then Jesus said, "Open, you massive gate; and you winds, bear it away so that it may return no more." The gate then disappeared, and Jesus moved His right hand over the silent slumberers, saying, "This dust will awake; it will be quickened and prepared for the habitation of disembodied spirits."

A voice inquired, "How will these awake? How will the grave give up the dead?" It was Justice, who appeared above the gateway.

Then Jesus arose from the tomb, holding in His hand the keys of the dark dominions. A voice spoke from a cloud that rested above the scene, saying, *"This is My beloved Son'* (Matt. 3:17), *'the Hope of Israel'* (Jer. 14:8), *'the Bright and Morning Star'* (Rev. 22:16). Peace be to the world."

The cloud then descended, and as it approached Jesus, Mercy moved from it. Addressing Justice, Mercy said, "This is the Offering I bring, and this is the trophy of His victory, even the body of Jesus now raised from the tomb and made immortal. Do you, Justice, accept the Offering?"

Justice replied, "The Offering is accepted. Divine power has immortalized the outer man, giving life to that from which life had departed."

Then said Mercy, "The Offering arises in perfection, animated with divine life, and will be glorified from this point forward. In Jesus, the divine Spirit came to seek and save perverted man (see Luke 19:10), even as a faithful shepherd seeks the lost sheep that has strayed from the fold. (See Matthew 18:12.) Henceforth, salvation will be preached to the forlorn race, and hope, like a star of superior light, will guide the wanderer to the port of peace. Jesus controls the fury of discordant elements; they will no longer drive the humble mariner to the regions of eternal night. The mighty watchman who, by divine appointment, guards the cold sepulchre remains at the gateway of death. Heaven has determined that death will give up her dead in the Last Day—that appointed Day when God will make up His jewels (Mal. 3:17 KJV) and will spare all who love and obey Him, even as a man spares his own son who serves him."

Then Justice, addressing Jesus, said, "You are from everlasting to everlasting, King of Kings and Lord of Lords. You have the keys of death. Heaven accepts the Offering and acknowledges the victory. Your mission, trial, and conquest are inscribed upon the throne of eternal recollection. The cross is now forever engraved upon and worked throughout all things in the kingdom of righteousness—to be kept in everlasting remembrance. Behold, I come to You, Lamb slain for sinners—yes, You upon whose shoulders rests the government of peace (Isa. 9:6). I embrace You. You are God." Having said this, Justice embraced Jesus.

Mercy then said, "Will the sinner, even he who lies in his fallen condition, be rescued? Will he find favor?"

Justice replied, "God in Christ reconciles the world to Himself (2 Cor. 5:19). Through His mediation, heaven will be just in the justification of all who come to God through Him. If the sinner forsakes the evil of his ways, and if the unrighteous man forsakes his thoughts and returns to the Lord, he will obtain favor. (See Isaiah 55:7.) He who seeks life will, in Jesus, enjoy the blessings of everlasting righteousness and peace." (See Isaiah 32:17.)

Then Mercy, raising her hands and eyes to heaven, said, "Now salvation is complete. From now on, Your glory, O God, shines upon the fallen planet. Your name will be adored by all who have blessed immortality, because You have provided the means for the salvation of man."

Having said this, Mercy also embraced Jesus, and a cloud of light encompassed them. With this cloud, and amid the hallelujahs of legions, Jesus arose from the tomb. Justice and Mercy then blended into the sphere of the Lord so as to lose their identity, and they were thereafter only revealed in the person of Jesus.

The Ascension

Before us now appeared the afflicted disciples who, having met on a mountain by special appointment of their Lord (Matt. 28:16), were communing with each other concerning the Resurrection. Suddenly a light shone upon them, and Jesus appeared in their midst and said, "Fear not. *'All authority has been given to Me in heaven and on earth. Go therefore and make disciples of all the nations, baptizing them in the name of the Father and of the Son and of the Holy Spirit, teaching them to observe all things that I have commanded you; and lo, I am with you always, even to the end of the age'* (vv. 18–20). You will be persecuted by men for My name's sake, but I have overcome, and you will also overcome if you trust My Word. (See Matthew 5:11; John 16:33.)

'And these signs will follow those who believe: in My name they will cast out demons; they will speak with new tongues; they will take up serpents; and if they drink anything deadly, it will by no means hurt them; they will lay hands on the sick, and they will recover' (Mark 16:17–18). 'But tarry in the city of Jerusalem until you are endued with power from on high' (Luke 24:49)."

After this, He lifted up His hands and blessed them. While blessing them He arose, and a cloud received Him out of their sight (Acts 1:9).

Then a voice from the heavens, as of a mighty angel, said, "*Lift up your heads, O you gates! And be lifted up, you everlasting doors! And the King of glory shall come in*" (Ps. 24:7).

"*Who is this King of glory?*" (v. 8), inquired another from an opposite portion of the heavens.

The voice answered, "*The* LORD *strong and mighty, the* LORD *mighty in battle. Lift up your heads, O you gates! Lift up, you everlasting doors! And the King of glory shall come in*" (vv. 8–9).

Then the innumerable millions who filled the heavens swept the chords of their stringed instruments with strong hands, and with loud voices they said, "We give You thanks, O Lord God Almighty, who was, is, and is to come (Rev. 1:8), because You have taken to Yourself Your great power and have conquered. We praise You, O Lord, who are the King of Kings and Lord of Lords, the Alpha and Omega, the Beginning and the End, the First and the Last." (See Revelation 1:8; 22:13.)

Then the cloud arose into the heavens, and with it, the great congregation who attended the Ascension. As they arose, they still uttered, "You are holy,

O Lord God Almighty, who was, is, and is to come. Lift up your heads, you everlasting gates, and let the King of Glory come in. The Lord Redeemer is the King of Glory."

During the Ascension, the disciples had steadfastly looked up into the heavens where their arisen and ascended Lord had gone. But as the cloud that received Him from their sight finally disappeared, they worshipped Him. Afterward, they arose in silence and departed for Jerusalem.

chapter 20

The Rescue

❧

The former scenes having passed, we heard an angel proclaim with a loud voice, "Now salvation appears. Hope, you inhabitants of earth —yes, rejoice, for the Lion of the Tribe of Judah has *'prevailed to open the book, and to loose the seven seals thereof'* (Rev. 5:5 KJV). Let salvation, the Year of Jubilee, be proclaimed afar. Go forth, you messengers; declare the love of God as it has been manifested in the rescue of the bewildered race. Indeed, let the heavens echo the glad news that *'God so loved the world that He gave His only begotten Son, that whoever believes in Him should not perish but have everlasting life'* (John 3:16)."

As the angel spoke, we heard a voice of lamentation saying, *"O wretched man that I am! Who will deliver me from this body of death?"* (Rom. 7:24). From the direction of this voice arose a cloud that contained frightful tempests. A little beyond that cloud arose lofty mountains, whose very sides appeared to send forth fire and smoke in all the terrors of warring elements. Again the voice of bitter wailing said, "Must we perish?"

The dark cloud that hung over the scene parted, and we beheld, by the aid of a pale light, the forlorn man and his friends—the same ones displayed in a former scene. By them stood a man dressed in simple apparel. He was holding in his hand a book, from which he read, *"Come to Me, all you who labor and are heavy laden, and I will give you rest"* (Matt. 11:28). As he read, the afflicted man looked up, and although somewhat disturbed by his presence, said, "To whom may I go? In whom will I have hope?"

"In Jesus, who is the Savior of men," answered the messenger.

"But I am polluted from the sole of my foot to the crown of my head," continued the fallen man.

Then the messenger read from the book again, *"Though your sins are like scarlet, they shall be as white as snow; though they are red like crimson, they shall be as wool"* (Isa. 1:18).

The sufferer replied, *"I have sinned against heaven"* (Luke 15:18).

Again the messenger read, *"Let the wicked forsake his way, and the unrighteous man his thoughts; let him return to the LORD, and He will have mercy on him; and to our God, for He will abundantly pardon"* (Isa. 55:7). Then he said, "It is also written, *'Those who are well have no need of a physician, but those who are sick'* (Matt. 9:12). If you seek to enter into life with all your heart, you may. Look up," he continued, as he raised his hand, and immediately a light shone from above, revealing the Redeemer stretched upon the cross. The sufferer heard a voice saying, *" 'I am the way, the truth, and the life. No one comes to the Father except through Me'* (John 14:6). *'He who believes in Me, though he may die, he shall live. And whoever lives and believes in Me shall never die. Do you believe this?'* (John 11:25–26)."

The sufferer replied, *"Lord, I believe; help my unbelief!"* (Mark 9:24). Raising his hands, he prayed, *"God, be merciful to me a sinner!"* (Luke 18:13). A

178

light descended, resting upon him, and the Spirit of God pervaded his soul and said to his spirit, "Your sins have been forgiven, your guilt has been removed, and your wounds are healed. The Spirit quickens you, calling you to arise, for salvation has come to you."

Then the redeemed man arose, rejoicing and worshipping. The light that shone on him revealed his inner being, upon which was impressed the image of the cross. Upon his heart was written the law of heaven.

Again the messenger, who still stood near him, read, *"Blessed are the pure in heart, for they shall see God"* (Matt. 5:8). Addressing him, the messenger then said, "Quickened by the Spirit, you have passed from death to life (John 5:24); you are restored to harmony and clothed with the garments of salvation (Isa. 61:10). 'Go forth,' says the Spirit, 'proclaim the grace of God, by which you have been redeemed. The harvest is truly great, but the laborers are few (Matt. 9:37). Go, preach the Gospel, and seek the lost (Mark 16:15). Freely you have received, now freely give' (Matt. 10:8). This is the Spirit of the Gospel of the Lord our Redeemer. Be faithful to the grace given to you. Watch, that when your Lord comes and calls for you, you may give account of your stewardship" (Luke 16:1–13).

Then he read, "Behold! I am with you, to bless and strengthen you (Isa. 41:10). For every trial, my grace will be sufficient" (2 Cor. 12:9).

The redeemed man then raised his eyes to heaven and prayed, "Be my help, O God. I can do all things if Jesus Christ strengthens me" (Phil. 4:13). As a servant of the cross, an ambassador of Jesus, he entered the cloud that made dark and gloomy the plain at the foot of the mountain. And as he departed, we heard him say, *"'O LORD, truly I am Your servant...You have loosed my bonds....What shall I render to the LORD for all His benefits toward me?...I will offer to You the sacrifice of thanksgiving, and will call upon the name of the LORD. I will pay my vows to the LORD now in the presence of all His people'* (Ps. 116:16, 12, 17–18). *'Search me, O God, and know my heart; try me, and know my anxieties; and see if there is any wicked way in me, and lead me in the way everlasting'* (Ps. 139:23–24). *'Praise the LORD, all you Gentiles! Laud Him, all you peoples! For His merciful kindness is great toward us, and the truth of the LORD endures forever. Praise the LORD!'* (Ps. 117:1–2)."

Praises of the Redeemed

Then an innumerable company of redeemed spirits drew near and, led by Mary the mother of Jesus, chanted with loud voices, "We will praise You, O Lord God Almighty, who was, is, and is to come, for Your wondrous works with the children of men! *'Just and true are Your ways'* (Rev. 15:3), You Prince and Author of salvation! You have redeemed us. When we were not mindful of You, your Spirit sought us. Worthy is the Lamb! Wondrous are Your works, O You who dwell above the cherubim, whose throne is the eternity of cause, whose dominion is over all. Praise, glory, and dominion be to You throughout everlasting ages. Amen.

"We will lift up our voices to You! Your glory inspires, and the love You have granted to man who was fallen is now and will ever be the theme of our song. Amen!

"Praised be Your name, Most High! From our hearts go forth alleluias! You have redeemed us from sin, which has dominion over the fallen soul; and from death You have exalted us to the glory of divine abodes. Oh, praise God, you who with exalted voices may utter His holy name! Praise Him, you congregations of seraphim who adorn the pavilion of His throne. Yes, bow down before the majesty of His love by which He redeemed us! Let His name, who is the Prince and Savior, be mentioned with most profound reverence. Praise His name forever! Praise Him forever! Amen! To Him be glory, honor, and dominion evermore! Amen! Hallelujah!"

Finally, an angel addressed me and said, "These infants, having been prepared, will ascend to a more exalted plane. They will go to a realm where, blessed with superior advantages and surrounded by still brighter glories, they will arise from one degree of attainment to another and will bathe in ever flowing crystal waters. They will glide in crystalline barges over the smooth and transparent rivers and will gather fruit from the groves and flowering vines that always adorn the banks of those placid waters.

"The glory of that sphere descends, and those spirits who must lead these infants upward have received them from their former guardians. Let us arise."

chapter 21

The Return

The period now drew near when I was to return to the earth. The infants, their attending angels, and those who had been employed in the various scenes were congregated together. They sang a soft and melodious hymn, during which they fixed their attention on me. More than ever, I felt their love and the value of heaven and heavenly associations. At length, the spirit who had kissed the cross approached me, leading the two children, as on a former occasion, and addressed me with the following words:

"Marietta, for a season you are to leave us. We love you and deeply sympathize with you. You are beloved by all, but it is our Redeemer's pleasure that you return to earth, and we cheerfully submit. Marietta, we rejoice in the precious promise of your return at the appointed time."

"Yes, in this we rejoice," said the multitude.

"We rejoice also," continued the spirit, "because you have been permitted to visit these realms in spirit, to behold some of their beauties, and to realize the harmony and divine order of paradisical abodes and of angelic worship. Moreover, we praise our heavenly Father, because you have been permitted to witness the mode by which infants are instructed in the great truths of man's perverted nature, and also the means provided for man's redemption. It fills us with delight to know that you have not only been permitted to behold the Redeemer, but you have also been received and blessed by Him in whom we have life and through whom we obtain heaven. We will give you our spirit of love, and, as one, we will embrace you and patiently await the happy period when we will hail you at the gate of the Holy City upon your return."

Then all arose and encompassed me as in a dome of spirits. The spirit who had addressed me pressed me to her heart, and I felt their influences as the embrace of one. When I look back on that scene now, my soul is filled with ecstasy, and to attempt to describe it is in vain.

After this manifestation of love, the spirit led the two children to me. They entwined their holy arms around my neck, pressed kiss after kiss upon my lips, and said, "Marietta, when you are again with those in the outer world who love us and who have mourned our loss, tell them we are happy, that we have no sorrow. We are ever with our guardians. We love all, and Jesus our Redeemer above all. Tell them we will await their arrival here with patience. We love you, Marietta, and will meet you again."

They once more embraced me and then withdrew. The spirit who had led them to me said, "Marietta, trust your Redeemer evermore. Relate on earth the story of redemption. Do well your work of love."

* * *

Then Jesus descended from a cloud. Placing His hand upon my head, He spoke to me, saying, "Child, for a wise purpose you are to return. Be faithful to your obligation. Relate, as you are able, what you have seen and heard. Fulfill your mission, and, at the appointed time, angels will meet you at the gate of death and bear you to mansions in the kingdom of peace. Do not be sad; My grace will sustain you. In your sufferings you will be supported." Then an angel gave Him a golden goblet, and He placed it to my lips. As I drank I was filled with new life and fortitude to endure the separation, and I bowed and worshipped Him.

With His right hand, He raised me up and said, "Child of sorrow from a world of gloom, you are redeemed, you are blessed forevermore. Be faithful, and when your course on earth has ended, you will enter into the joy of your Lord." Then placing in my hand an olive branch, He said, "Bear this to earth, as you have been instructed." Again he laid His hand upon my head, and light and love filled my spirit.

The time had come for my departure. I looked around at the scenes of that lovely city and at its happy inhabitants. I offered myself in thanksgiving to God for the blessings of immortality and, above all, for the gift of grace in Jesus, who is the Redeemer. Before the multitudes, I lifted my hands to my Lord and my voice in prayer for support in that hour, so that I might be kept in the love of Him who had blessed me. Then I was carried in the arms of angels to the gateway of the temple, where I had first met the Lord. From there, while angels chanted praise to God and the Lamb, I descended to earth with my former guide. Entering the room where my body lay, I soon awoke.

The Return

Patiently I await the hour that I know is determined, when I will go back and enjoy the fruition of those realms of bliss where my spirit obtained its assurance of joys to come. I will praise my heavenly Father for my hope in Jesus, which is worth ten thousand worlds to me. And when I arrive in paradise, free from mortality, I will praise Him with an undivided and pure heart and with holy lips. There I will, in loud anthems, exalt the name of my Redeemer while eternity endures.

All of Grace
Charles H. Spurgeon

Charles Spurgeon outlines the plan of salvation in such clear, simple language that everyone can understand and be drawn to the Father. Any attempt to please God based upon our own works brings only self-righteousness and coldness of heart, but God's free grace makes the heart glow with thankfulness for His love. This classic is summed up in Spurgeon's final cry to the reader, "Meet me in heaven!"

ISBN: 978-0-88368-857-1 • Trade • 176 pages

WHITAKER HOUSE

www.whitakerhouse.com

A Place Called Heaven
E. M. Bounds

Christ has gone to prepare a place for you in heaven!
Examining the Scriptures that pertain to heaven, author
E. M. Bounds reveals how you can look forward to receiving
your crown of glory, reigning with Christ forever, and
reuniting with your loved ones. Get a taste of heaven here
on earth, learn a true Christian attitude toward eternity,
and discover how to lay up treasures in your eternal home.
Through Bound's anointed writing, the breathtaking beauty
and joy that await every believer in Christ will become real
to you. You can know that you are heaven-bound!

ISBN: 978-0-88368-958-5 • Trade • 160 pages

www.whitakerhouse.com

Smith Wigglesworth on Heaven
Smith Wigglesworth

Illustrating his insights with many dramatic, real-life examples, Smith Wigglesworth has a dynamic message in store for those who are looking toward the Second Coming. He explains how to prepare for your future in eternity with God while experiencing the power and joy of the Holy Spirit in the present. Discover God's plans for you in this life and what He has in store for you in heaven. You can know victorious living—now and for all eternity.

ISBN: 978-0-88368-954-7 • Trade • 224 pages

WHITAKER HOUSE

www.whitakerhouse.com

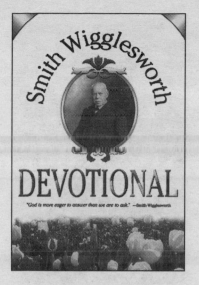

Smith Wigglesworth Devotional
Smith Wigglesworth

You are invited to journey with Smith Wigglesworth on a year-long trip that will quench your spiritual thirst while it radically transforms your faith. As you daily explore these challenging insights from the Apostle of Faith, you will connect with God's glorious power, cast out doubt, and see impossibilities turn into realities. Your prayer life will never be the same again when you personally experience the joy of seeing awesome, powerful results as you extend God's healing grace to others.

ISBN: 978-0-88368-574-7 • Trade • 560 pages

WHITAKER HOUSE

www.whitakerhouse.com

The Soulwinner
Charles H. Spurgeon

When Jesus returned to heaven, He left us with a mission—continue His work of bringing lost souls home to the Father. Charles Spurgeon accepted this mission and personally escorted thousands of people into the saving knowledge of Jesus Christ. In this book, he crystallizes the wisdom and experience of a lifetime as a soulwinner.

"If you are eager for real joy, I am persuaded that no joy of growing wealthy, no joy of influence over your fellow creatures, no joy of any other sort, can ever compare with the rapture of saving a soul from death."
—C. H. Spurgeon

ISBN: 978-0-88368-709-3 • Trade • 304 pages

www.whitakerhouse.com

Heaven Awaits
D. L. Moody

"How can I get to heaven?"

This question is asked by millions of people today. Help, encouragement, and definite answers await the reader, as page after page unfolds with the explanation of this exciting place—heaven—and how we can get there. With tremendous insight, D. L. Moody, a dynamic evangelist who reached thousands of people throughout the world with his special message of Christ's love, offers easy to understand explanations that make this book one that must be read and shared with others.

ISBN: 978-1-60374-036-4 • Pocket • 160 pages

WHITAKER HOUSE

www.whitakerhouse.com

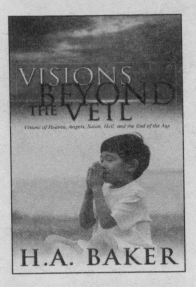

Visions Beyond the Veil
H. A. Baker

Beggars…Outcasts…Homeless…Such were the forgotten, uneducated children in China where the Spirit of God fell upon their humble orphanage, the Adullam Home. The boys spent days in powerful meetings, praying and praising God. Under the anointing of the Spirit, they prophesied and saw visions. Discover how angels operate and protect us, the fate of unbelievers, what happens when we die, what our jobs will be like in heaven, and much more as paradise is revealed through the eyes of these precious children.

ISBN: 978-0-88368-786-4 • Trade • 192 pages

www.whitakerhouse.com